IFIP Advances in Information and Communication Technology 599

Editor-in-Chief

Kai Rannenberg, Goethe University Frankfurt, Germany

Editorial Board Members

IFIP – The International Federation for Information Processing

IFIP was founded in 1960 under the auspices of UNESCO, following the first World Computer Congress held in Paris the previous year. A federation for societies working in information processing, IFIP's aim is two-fold: to support information processing in the countries of its members and to encourage technology transfer to developing nations. As its mission statement clearly states:

IFIP is the global non-profit federation of societies of ICT professionals that aims at achieving a worldwide professional and socially responsible development and application of information and communication technologies.

IFIP is a non-profit-making organization, run almost solely by 2500 volunteers. It operates through a number of technical committees and working groups, which organize events and publications. IFIP's events range from large international open conferences to working conferences and local seminars.

The flagship event is the IFIP World Computer Congress, at which both invited and contributed papers are presented. Contributed papers are rigorously refereed and the rejection rate is high.

As with the Congress, participation in the open conferences is open to all and papers may be invited or submitted. Again, submitted papers are stringently refereed.

The working conferences are structured differently. They are usually run by a working group and attendance is generally smaller and occasionally by invitation only. Their purpose is to create an atmosphere conducive to innovation and development. Refereeing is also rigorous and papers are subjected to extensive group discussion.

Publications arising from IFIP events vary. The papers presented at the IFIP World Computer Congress and at open conferences are published as conference proceedings, while the results of the working conferences are often published as collections of selected and edited papers.

IFIP distinguishes three types of institutional membership: Country Representative Members, Members at Large, and Associate Members. The type of organization that can apply for membership is a wide variety and includes national or international societies of individual computer scientists/ICT professionals, associations or federations of such societies, government institutions/government related organizations, national or international research institutes or consortia, universities, academies of sciences, companies, national or international associations or federations of companies.

More information about this series at http://www.springer.com/series/6102

Mieczysław Lech Owoc ·
Maciej Pondel (Eds.)

Artificial Intelligence
for Knowledge Management

7th IFIP WG 12.6 International Workshop, AI4KM 2019
Held at IJCAI 2019
Macao, China, August 11, 2019
Revised Selected Papers

Springer

Editors
Mieczysław Lech Owoc ⓘ
Wroclaw University of Economics
and Business
Wroclaw, Poland

Maciej Pondel ⓘ
Wroclaw University of Economics
and Business
Wroclaw, Poland

ISSN 1868-4238   ISSN 1868-422X (electronic)
IFIP Advances in Information and Communication Technology
ISBN 978-3-030-85003-6   ISBN 978-3-030-85001-2 (eBook)
https://doi.org/10.1007/978-3-030-85001-2

This Springer imprint is published by the registered company Springer Nature Switzerland AG
The registered company address is: Gewerbestrasse 11, 6330 Cham, Switzerland

Preface

Welcome to the proceedings of the 7th IFIP WG 12.6 International Workshop on Artificial Intelligence for Knowledge Management (AI4KM 2019), which was held in conjunction with the 28th International Joint Conference on Artificial Intelligence (IJCAI 2019). IJCAI was held during August 10–16, 2019, in Macao, China, with AI4KM taking place on August 11, 2019.

The very rich program of IJCAI-19 covered a huge number of papers presenting different aspects of theoretical background as well as plenty of practical solutions in the artificial intelligence (AI) domain. In the main tracks of the conference topics such as the usability of graphs and networks, the exploration of potential resources in different domains, and learning as the crucial tool in discovering knowledge appeared very often. In addition, specialized co-located events, which were focused on improving human well-being through AI and understanding intelligence and human-level AI in the new machine learning era, proposed more global perspectives of modern intelligent technologies.

Knowledge management is a large multidisciplinary field having its roots in both management and AI. Knowledge is one of the intangible capitals that influence the performance of organizations and their capacity to innovate. Since the beginning of the KM movement in the early 1990s, companies and nonprofit organizations have experimented with various approaches. AI has brought additional knowledge modeling, knowledge processing, and problem-solving techniques. The AI4KM workshop aims to bridge the gap between AI and knowledge management to advance new methods for organizing, accessing, and exploiting multidisciplinary knowledge, bringing together both decision makers and the developers of intelligent technology.

AI4KM was initiated in Montpellier in 2012 as part of the European Conference on Artificial Intelligence (http://www.eccai.org/ecai.shtml), and it continued in Warsaw in 2014 as a part of the Conference on Knowledge Acquisition and Management (KAM) under the framework of the Federated Conferences on Computer Science and Information Systems (https://fedcsis.org/2014/kam). The third edition of the workshop, which took place in Buenos Aires in 2015, saw the beginning of the partnership with the International Joint Conference on Artificial Intelligence (https://ijcai-15.org), with further editions taking place in New York (2016), Melbourne (2017), and Stockholm (2018) – all under the IJCAI framework.

The objective of this multidisciplinary workshop is to gather both researchers and practitioners to discuss methodological, technical, and organizational aspects of AI used for knowledge management and to share the feedback on KM applications using AI. The main theme of AI4KM 2019 was "AI for Humans", focusing on AI applied to face current challenges such as climate change, eco-innovation, societal innovation, and global security.

This volume contains a selection of updated and extended papers from the workshop. The final versions of the papers cover new contributions in the research area concerning the use of AI methods and techniques for knowledge management.

Our invited speaker Waltraut Ritter addressed a very current topic: AI in transportation. Presentations of solutions, discovered obstacles, and perspectives from different countries allowed us to better understand the importance of AI techniques in the discussed field.

In the first presented paper, "Using a Semantic-based Support System for Merging from Process Participants", the authors proposed a useful system for managing knowledge about business processes which helps in complex cases.

The quest of applying a new approach addressed to smart cities management was discussed in "The Concept of Crowdsourcing in Knowledge Management in Smart Cities", where the author developed a model of distribution of knowledge between residents and decision makers.

Smart city management supported by big data technology oriented on crucial agglomeration components was discussed in the second paper on smart cities, "The Impact of Big Data in Smart City Concepts".

The authors of the paper "Artificial Intelligence Technologies in Education: Benefits, Strategies and Implementation in Non-Public Universities" presented an overview of the state of the art and proposals for the implementation of intelligent technologies in the specific sector of education, including administration as well as teaching.

Similar to the previous paper, in terms of the implementation area, was the presentation on "E-learning as an Extending Tool of Knowledge Management" where the author demonstrated relationships essential to the consideration of knowledge management and e-learning.

The importance of associated AI technologies (in this case IoT) for business was addressed in the paper "Internet of Things as a Significant Factor of Innovations for Intelligent Organizations", which specified business models determined by the discussed technology.

The problem of presenting retrieved information in a smarter way for broadly defined managerial purposes was discussed in the paper "Semantics Visualization as a User Interface in Business Information Searching".

In the paper "Machine Learning Solutions in Retail E-commerce to Increase Marketing Efficiency" the authors proposed a method of machine learning-based data analysis leading to tailored offers for customers.

In summary, the papers presented at AI4KM 2019 and included in this proceedings cover a range of novel AI methods in KM development, and we hope that you will enjoy reading and disseminating the papers.

We would like to thank the members of the Program Committee, who reviewed the papers and created the opportunity to manage an interesting workshop in Macao. We would also like to express our gratitude to all the authors and our invited speaker, Waltraut Ritter from Knowledge Dialogues, Hong Kong. Our special thanks go to Eunika Mercier-Laurent (the chair of IFIP TC-12 "Artificial Intelligence") for her contribution to the organization and kindly coordinating the entire project. Finally, our thanks are addressed to the Local Organizing Committee and all the supporting institutions.

December 2020

Mieczysław Lech Owoc
Maciej Pondel

Organization

Program Chairs

Mieczysław Lech Owoc   Wrocław University of Economics and Business,
                          Poland
Maciej Pondel   Wrocław University of Economics and Business,
                          Poland

Program Committee

Weronika T. Adrian   University of Calabria, Italy
Danielle Boulanger   Lyon 3 University, France
Otthein Herzog   Universität Bremen, Germany
Knut Hinkelmann   University of Applied Sciences, Switzerland
Gülgün Kayakutlu   ITU Istanbul, Turkey
Antoni Ligęza   AGH University of Science and Technology Krakow,
                          Poland
Helena Lindskog   Linköping University, Sweden
Dickson Lucose   GCS Agile, Australia
Nada Matta   University of Technology of Troyes, France
Daniel O'Leary   USC Marshall SB, USA
Maciej Pondel   Wrocław University of Economics and Business,
                          Poland
Vincent Ribiere   IKI, Thailand
Frederique Segond   Viseo, France
Eric Tsui   The Hong Kong Polytechnic University, Hong Kong
Caroline Wintergerst   Lyon 3 University, France

Local Organizing Committee

Eunika Mercier-Laurent   University of Reims Champagne-Ardenne, France
Mieczysław L. Owoc   Wrocław University of Economics and Business,
                          Poland
Waltraut Ritter   Knowledge Dialogues, Hong Kong

Contents

Using a Semantic-Based Support System for Merging Knowledge from Process Participants

Krzysztof Kluza[1]([⊠]), Mateusz Kagan[1], Piotr Wiśniewski[1], Weronika T. Adrian[1], Paweł Jemioło[1], Anna Suchenia[2], and Antoni Ligęza[1]

[1] AGH University of Science and Technology, al. A. Mickiewicza 30, 30-059 Krakow, Poland
kluza@agh.edu.pl
[2] Cracow University of Technology, ul. Warszawska 24, 31-155 Kraków, Poland

Abstract. High complexity of business processes is a continually growing problem in real-life organisations. Hence, modelling a workflow poses a challenge for different participants. Many methods have been proposed for automatic generation of process models. This paper aims at presenting an approach for uniting knowledge from a number of stakeholders. In essence, a collection of tabular tasks definitions are combined into one classification of unordered activities. Later, semantic analysis of the input definitions is suggested in order to fuse them based on similarity of parameters. Using a set of predefined constraints and a dedicated construction algorithm, the resulting spreadsheet-based structure can then be converted into a model of a process.

1 Introduction

Business Process Management (BPM) is an area of research that deals with processes. Such processes describe how work is carried out in an enterprise to boost overall performance [1]. The exact definition of such an improvement depends on the nature and the scope of the specific organization, but usually it involves reduction of cost, execution times or error levels. One can accomplish this by redesigning or eliminating unproductive structures, reducing redundancies and transforming the processes. Business Process Models are thus used widely in BPM strategies aiming at making the work in a company less complicated.

Every business process can be depicted in various ways, i.e. workflows or diagrams [2]. Thanks to the Business Process Model, formalization of business processes is also possible. Business Process Models can help with process enhancement, or process verification, or process stimulation [3]. Nevertheless, its main aim is to enable better understanding of the business processes for involved people. While it does not seem complicated on the surface, modelling a process requires a great deal of data about a process. Acquiring such data is a challenging task, which can be tackled using Knowledge Engineering methods.

The main goal of Knowledge Engineering (KE) is providing solutions for acquisition and representation of knowledge in the unified form [4]. Its core field of study is called

M. L. Owoc and M. Pondel (Eds.): AI4KM 2019, IFIP AICT 599, pp. 1–16, 2021.
https://doi.org/10.1007/978-3-030-85001-2_1

Knowledge Acquisition (KA). It focuses on developing tools and methods facilitating the collection of knowledge from domain experts, as well as its later validation [5]. Knowledge Engineers often collaborate with Software Engineers in order to develop sophisticated Information Technology (IT) solutions.

Software Engineering (SE), in turn, is a discipline that refers to the production of software, beginning from the specification of the system to its maintenance [6], including all the intermediate steps. Opposite to software development, SE is concerned with solutions that are way more complex. It also tackle additional phases during the process of creation of the product comparing to software development. The holy grail of SE is to deliver products which are characterized by high quality.

Because business process can affect costs and delivery time of both services and goods, they remain a critical part of any enterprise. What is more, they can assess an organization's ability to adjust or adapt to new circumstances. It is thus essential for an organization to be aware of the mentioned dependencies. However, business processes have not long been properly understood and only recently gained attention they deserved. Henceforth, initiatives aiming at improving companies' processes have been started worldwide. One must understand that what matters most is the necessity of thorough comprehension of what exactly specific process depicts. Therefore, improving a process has to be preceded by active data collection, then, modelling it to the form of workflows and graphs. Afterwards, process analyst using methods developed by software engineers is able to shift time constraints and simplify the process. It can be achieved thanks to providing standards for interoperability [7] or generating models from text and documents [8] and from spreadsheets [9]. Because spreadsheets are used by most of the companies, this last approach remains particularly interesting. Such a method draws from the concept of Constraint Solving Problem. After transforming spreadsheet with tasks that were run within a process to a proper format, the solution is generated. Then, a Process Model is formed using methods called Model Construction or Process Mining. Such a model is encoded using XML and therefore can be easily improved in the future. Despite taking care of generating a model from previously acquired data, this concept does not tackle the need for gathering information and possible inconsistencies, i.e. contradictory or duplicated items. Such elements have to be addressed manually by business process analysts.

This paper aims at presenting an approach for business analysts which can offer assistance with the laborious task of consolidating gathered pieces of information about business processes into a uniform spreadsheet. Using such a spreadsheet, it is later possible to generate a process model. We thus reckon that our tool would enable users to save time that is needed to organize information about business processes. This paper extends our research presented and discussed during AI4KM 2019 workshop [10].

The method discussed in this paper constitutes a phase in a more complex general approach that automates process and decision model generation. This general approach is presented in Fig. 1, where the method discussed in this paper is highlighted (in red).

This general approach is based on a concept of process modelling with spreadsheets [11], in which a process model can be generated from a spreadsheet. In the approach, another option is to use an existing knowledge specification, like Attribute Relationship Diagrams (ARD) [12], which is a knowledge representation method for structured

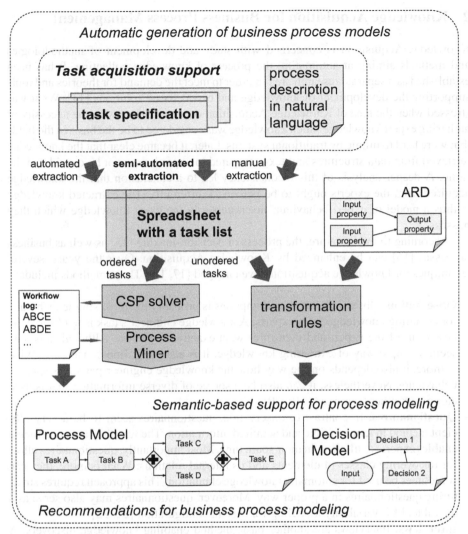

Fig. 1. Outline of the methodology proposed for the automated generation of business processes and business decisions.

specification of a system. From such a specification, it is possible to generate a business process model integrated with a decision model [13].

The rest of the paper is organized as follows. In Sect. 2, we discuss the origins and the key concepts regarding Knowledge Acquisition. We also provide an overview of tools used to gather knowledge about business processes. Section 3 focuses on the details of the proposed method for integrating knowledge based on users specifications. Then, in Sect. 5, we investigate the results of the test carried out on an exemplary process data. The paper ends with Sect. 6, where we summarize our work and outline our future ideas.

2   Knowledge Acquisition for Business Process Management

Knowledge Acquisition is concerned with study and development of methodologies and methods aiming at automating the process of knowledge collecting. It has been established as a separate research area in order to meet the demand for theories and tools supporting the development of knowledge and expert-based solutions [14]. What was stressed when the area of Knowledge Acquisition was established, was the necessity of gathering expert knowledge. Such knowledge was considered to be the basis in the fields that were hard to mimic by traditional systems. Later, it became clear that the knowledge retrieved from data structures and text compared to expertise cannot be considered the same. A deeper analysis of this inconsistency led to a conclusion that the knowledge acquired from the experts ought to be perceived differently. The extracted knowledge is thus a model of expert behaviour, not necessarily the exact knowledge which they possess.

According to the literature, the process of decision-making [15] as well as business processes [16] can be enhanced by Knowledge Acquisition. Over the years, several techniques for knowledge acquisition have emerged [17, 18]. These methods include:

- **Observation.** Observation in its assumptions is probably the most simple technique for acquiring knowledge from experts. A knowledge engineer's task is to observe the behaviour of the expert and then infer what exactly they know. Although this may seem a simple way of extracting knowledge, it is also very time-consuming. What is more, it also depends on the way how the knowledge engineer perceives specific behaviours. Nevertheless, it can also be a source of diverse information that is used along with other techniques [19, 20].
- **Questionnaires.** In contrast to observation, questionnaires seem to be a very efficient method in terms of time and acquired information. The way they are constructed enables experts to fill them in their spare time. Most importantly, questionnaires allow for uncovering classes of elements and its internal relations. What is more, they can sometimes be used for automatic knowledge elicitation. This approach requires structuring questionnaires in a proper way. Moreover, questionnaires may also serve as a useful tool for variability modeling for system configuration [21, 22].
- **Interviews.** Interviews are another basic method enabling knowledge discovery. A knowledge engineer poses several questions about the process and an expert's task is to pass the knowledge to their investigator. Such a conversation may reveal details about the process or a particular task. Like observation, this method is very naive and it can also be time-consuming for all people involved, especially when numerous iterations of interviews are envisioned. Development of models by business analysts may be supported by using the existing domain patterns [23–25] or recommendation tools [26–28].
- **Automatic Knowledge Acquisition.** Contrary to the previously enumerated methods, this one is meant for detecting knowledge from a digital source, namely documents, reports and logs. One of its field of application is risk identification and management [29]. This way of handling data is very domain-specific. It also depends on the amount of available information. Although it might provide a neat overview of a particular

domain, it may also fail to acquire knowledge when relevant data is missing. Additionally, it might take some time for a system to gather enough information in order to start knowledge elicitation. If there are existing event logs, various process mining techniques may be used [30]. However, not always complete logs are available, and sometimes even process mining requires acquiring knowledge from multiple process participants [31].

When talking about BPM purposes, Knowledge Acquisition is highly useful at an early stage of model creation. It can be applied when one wants to acquire information about the process before its modelling. Among methods incorporated by business analysts, there are all those mentioned above. Plenty of other strategies are also developed particularly for BPM initiatives, e.g. document analysis and workshops. The first one focuses on using information about processes derived from existing documentation within a company. According to the state-of-the-art paper [32], there is a variety of solutions in mining process models from natural language description, from these based on form of structured text (use cases [33], group stories [34]), to the general descriptions in natural language [8, 35].

On the other hand, workshops gather knowledge engineers, process analysts, together with experts. Then, by discussion and other forms of collaboration, they develop a common Business Process Model. It can thus be considered as an extended version of interviews. What is more, triangulation techniques are often applied. It means that several methods are used in order to acquire knowledge, i.e. filling out questionnaires in between interview sessions. There are various ways of supporting collective decision making [36]. Using interactive technologies during workshops may improve participant involvement as well as improve the quality of outcomes [37]. Another important issue is when to stop the meetings as at some point the models may not be improved any further i.e. more workshops do not necessarily lead to better models [38]. To sum up, Knowledge Acquisition is key when talking about modelling of a process or other BPM tasks in general.

3 Similarity Assessment of Collected Specifications

Our method is designed to facilitate knowledge acquired from domain experts by examining the similarities between different tasks within the process. We distinguished two main requirements. First of all, the system ought to allow for the smart integration of data provided by various users. Mediation in regards to specific data is also necessary. Secondly, data provided by different users should enable the system to generate a spreadsheet with a declarative process specification. The business analyst could then use such an output for creating BPMN process model.

To meet specified requirements, we introduced a comparing tool to our systems. It enables comparison of tasks due to statistical algorithms. The algorithms calculate the rate of similarity between data entities and tasks. Additionally, they base on the semantically-oriented dictionary of English, WordNet [39]. In WordNet, concepts and their synonyms are called WordNet synsets. The definitions are connected and form a hierarchy. Some of the concepts, called root synsets or unique beginners, are very general, i.e. State, Entity and Event. Moreover, other concepts may not even have a synonym in English dictionary. NLTK[1] contains the English WordNet, with 155,287 words and 117,659 synonym sets [39].

Each part of the task is compared individually because of differences between roles and standardization of a particular task. We thus compare:

- **Data Created and Data Required**. Data Attributes and Data Names are handled separately. Firstly, to calculate the similarity between the names of the Data, synonyms of such names are acquired through WordNet. Then an algorithm finds the intersection between these two sets. Afterwards, following formula is applied:

$$1 - \frac{1.4}{(0.4x+1.14)^{2.8}}$$

where x represents the size of mentioned intersection. The output of this formula is a number between 0 and 1. Such a function has a shape similar to a logarithmic one. When the name is not present in the WordNet, the Levenshtein distance is applied:

$$1 - \frac{m}{l}$$

where m is the length of the longest of the two words and the l represents the Levenshtein distance between these words.
- **Similarity between individual attributes of data** is handled using the same method that was applied to measure similarity between Data names.
- **Similarity between sets of entities**, i.e. data or attributes is determined as follows:

1. First, a similarity matrix is formed (see Table 1). Its columns consist of one set of entities, and rows represent the other set. Every intersecting cell comprises information about the similarity between these two units.
2. Next, the greatest value is found in such a matrix.
3. The greatest value is then added to the total similarity value.
4. Next, row and column comprising this value are removed from the matrix.
5. Steps 2–4 are repeated till the similarity matrix is empty.
6. In the end, total similarity value is divided by the size of the greater of the sets in order to calculate the similarity between the sets of entities.

Table 1. Similarity matrix. Each cell represents the ratio of similarity between the words in the column and the row.

	Purchase	Bill	funds
Invoice	0.28	0.74	0.17
Order	0.93	0.21	0.43
Assets	0.14	0.21	0.71

---
[1] The Natural Language Toolkit, see https://www.nltk.org/.

The workflow of the described algorithm is depicted in Fig. 2.

Fig. 2. Flowchart of the algorithm used for measuring the similarity between two sets of units.

– **Description.** Since it is the least structured aspect of a task, the exact way of comparing it has proved to be difficult to come up with. We thus use the naive approach, with the Cosine similarity as a metric. Firstly, each sentence is represented as a vector comprising numbers that correspond to the occurrences of each word from both sentences. Then, the angle between these vectors is calculated.

Once all partial similarity scores are determined for a pair of tasks, the result is the mean of all of those similarity scores estimated.

4 Implementation of a Merger System

The main goal of the system presented in this paper is to help a process analyst that facilitates knowledge gathered from domain experts with an analysis of similarity between different tasks within the process. The system should enable smart merging of the data provided by different users, as well as mediation with respect to specific data. The result should be a declarative process specification in a form of a spreadsheet based on data gathered from different users that could be used as a base for BPMN process model generation. Figure 3 presents a set of use cases for the designed system.

4.1 Merger System Architecture

The system is constructed in a client-server architecture where client is designed to operate independently relying on server only for advanced computing. Figure 4 shows an overview of the system and its main components:

– Spreadsheet Creator is used for creating a spreadsheet.
– Spreadsheet Merger is used for merging previously created spreadsheets.
– Spreadsheet Validator offers service for spreadsheet validation in terms of task duplications and data entities misuse.
– Spreadsheet Merger Assistance offers a web service that searches for duplications of a specific task.
– Task Comparator is used to calculate similarity index between two tasks.
– Wordnet API is a module that queries information from the Wordnet.

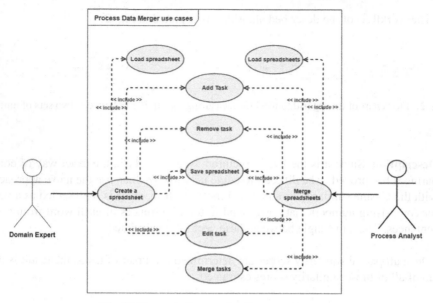

Fig. 3. Use case diagram for the merger system.

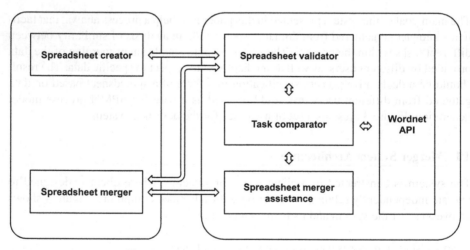

Fig. 4. Overview of the systems architecture.

4.2 Technology Stack

The overview of the technology stack is presented in Fig. 5. The technology stack for the client application consists mostly of JavaScript libraries in the Node.js environment as well as as tools for code inspection and code compiling. The technology stack of the server-side of the system consists of several modules in Python environment that create API for more advanced calculations.

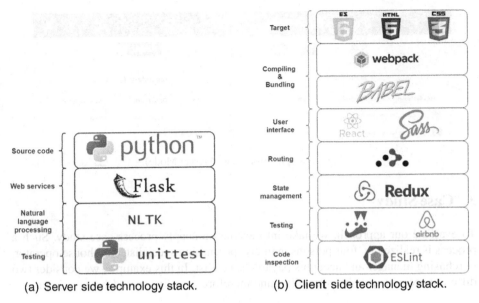

(a) Server side technology stack.　　　　(b) Client side technology stack.

Fig. 5. Technology stack.

4.3 User Interface

The application contains a web user interface which can work in two modes. In the "Creator Mode" (as seen in Fig. 6), the application contains only a list of tasks which can be edited and validated. In the "Merger Mode" (as presented in Fig. 7), the interface is split into two parts, each consisting of a single list of tasks. The list on the left-hand side is the main list of tasks, and it can be saved into a.csv file. The secondary list, on the right hand side, serves as a buffer for all tasks collected from domain experts. The tasks from both lists can be moved to the other one, highlighted, deleted or checked for duplicates in both lists. A user can also edit any task from both lists.

Fig. 6. Application view (Creator Mode).

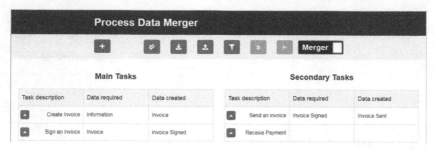

Fig. 7. Application view (Merger Mode).

5 Case Study

To evaluate our approach, we take into account a supply process case study. Such a process is realized by four persons, namely: purchasing specialist, warehouse operator, purchasing manager and accounts payable specialist. In this example, we consider two different accounts payable specialists and therefore have five spreadsheets as input.

Table 2. Activities performed by the first accounts payable specialist.

Task description	Data required	Data created
Reserve funds	Order reviewed	Funds reserved
Receive invoice	Invoice	Invoice
Record invoice	Invoice	Invoice recorded
Release funds	Invoice recorded, packing slip recorded	Funds released

Analysis of the first of the accounts payable specialists (see Table 2) with similarity threshold set to 65% showed that some of the data created and required are used only once. What is more, the tasks "Receive Invoice" and "Record Invoice" are probably too similar. Data required and data created are most often identical. Only slight differences can be observed sometimes. Being in such a situation process analyst might contact a domain expert to establish why is the spreadsheet constructed in this way. Additionally, it can be also profitable to inspect other spreadsheets to find a solution.

Table 3. Activities performed by the second accounts payable specialist.

Task description	Data required	Data created
Issue payment	Funds discharged	Order completed
Report invoice	Invoice	Invoice reported
Discharge funds	Invoice reported, packing-slip reported	Funds discharged
Receive invoice	Order sent	Invoice

Following this, we can use the second accounts payable specialist's spreadsheet (see Table 3) to resolve the mentioned issues. First, we can start by looking for duplicates of tasks "Receive invoice" in both spreadsheets. Again we set the similarity threshold to 65%. As an output, we get "Report Invoice" and "Receive Invoice". Because the tasks duplicate themselves, we can now merge them into one. By doing so, we remove redundancy. "Invoice" is set for data created and "Order created" for data required. Then we look for unique tasks within both spreadsheets. Such a task is "Issue Payment", and we move it to the main table. Next, we check if some tasks are similar to the task "Report invoice" from the second spreadsheet. In such a case, there is one task that can be considered similar. It is called "Record Invoice" in the first spreadsheet. These tasks are very likely to be the same, different names being the only difference. An analogous situation takes places when talking about tasks "Discharge funds" and "Release funds". However, we still do not know which version of the tasks is used by other people in their spreadsheets. We thus leave them all and will decide about it later.

Table 4. Activities performed by the purchasing manager.

Task description	Data required	Data created
Review order	Order created checked	Order reviewed
Send order	Funds reserved	Order sent

Table 5. Activities performed by the purchasing specialist.

Task description	Data required	Data created
Create order	Inventory checked	Order created
Reprocess order	Order reviewed	Order reprocessed

Table 6. Activities performed by the warehouse operator.

Task description	Data required	Data created
Check inventory	Goods-request	Inventory checked
Receive packing slip	Order sent	Packing slip
Record packing slip	Packing-slip	Packing slip

Afterwards, we take into account the spreadsheet created by the purchasing specialist (see Table 5). All of the tasks are unique. We can thus move them into the main table.

Next, we consider tasks in a spreadsheet from a purchasing manager (see Table 4). Once again, we can move all of them into the main table because they are all unique.

Eventually, we analyse a spreadsheet generated by the warehouse operator (see Table 6). Firstly, we establish that tasks "Receive Packing-slip" and "Check inventory" are unique. We thus move them into the main table. The task "Record Packing-slip" is unique too. However, both data required and created are the same. Therefore, it seems that something is missing in the spreadsheet. To tackle this issue, we have to look at specific tasks. We establish that two tasks use "Packing-slip" as their input, namely "Discharge funds" and "Release funds". In our example, data created by the "Discharge funds" is used whereas the output from "Release funds" is not. We can, therefore, move "Discharge funds" to the main table and remove the other task. Now, we can perform two fixes. Firstly, the tasks "Record packing-slip" are set to create data entity "Packing-slip reported". Secondly, we rename "Packing-slip reported" to "Report packing-slip" and move it to the main table. Additionally, we move the task "Report invoice" into the main table.

Task description	Data required	Data created
Reserve funds	Order Reviewed	Funds Reserved
Issue payment	Funds Discharged	Order Completed
Report invoice	Invoice	Invoice Reported
Discharge funds	Invoice Reported, Packing-slip Reported	Funds Discharged
Receive invoice	Order Sent	Invoice
Review Order	Order Created	Order Reviewed
Send Order	Funds Reserved	Order Sent
Create Order	Inventory Checked	Order Created
Reprocess Order	Order Reviewed	Order Reprocessed
Check inventory	Goods-request	Inventory Checked
Receive packing slip	Order Sent	Packing-slip
Report packing slip	Packing-slip	Packing-slip Reported

Fig. 8. Final version of the spreadsheet.

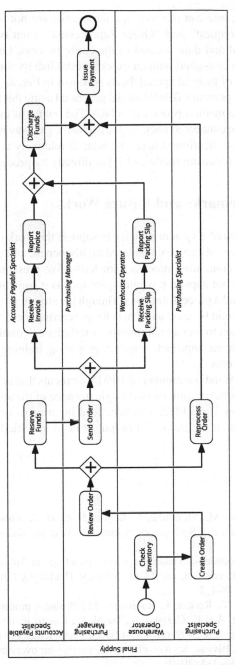

Fig. 9. Model of the supply case generated using our approach

As a general note, one can observe that three units are not used, namely: "Order Completed", "Goods-request" and "Order Reprocessed". First two of them are most probably data received and data created of the entire process. On the other hand, the third entity ought to be consulted with an expert to establish its connection to the whole process. Final version of merged spreadsheets is shown in Fig. 8.

At the very end, we present a BPMN model generated using this final spreadsheet (see Fig. 9). We base on the method proposed in [40]. The output of the "Reprocess Order" task should probably be connected back via the exclusive gateway to the "Review Order" task. Though it must be mentioned here, the issue is relatively minor. It can be easily fixed using automated repairing methods [41] or directly by process analyst.

6   Concluding Remarks and Future Works

In this paper, we presented a system which can support the work of a business analyst. We believe that our method can be considered highly beneficial thanks to the ability to generate spreadsheets containing process knowledge. We presented results using case study. We also pointed out gaps in this intelligent tool as it sometimes lacks the insight of the domain expert and a process analysts. Though the structure of the proposed model is not fully accurate, it can be used as a basis for generating the final solution.

In the future, we want to focus on improving similarity calculation by using machine learning models. Such an approach requires preparing training sets based on data collected from the systems.

We also intend to extend the number of BPMN elements that are supported. Besides, support for real-time collaboration on one single instance of the spreadsheet is required for practical application. It could also be beneficial in terms of time needed to resolve inconsistencies [42] about the input and output of tasks specified by various business experts.

References

1. Dumas, M., La Rosa, M., Mendling, J., Reijers, H.A., et al.: Fundamentals of Business Process Management, vol. 1. Springer, Heidelberg (2013). https://doi.org/10.1007/978-3-662-56509-4
2. Vaisman, A.: An introduction to business process modeling. In: Aufaure, M.-A., Zimányi, E. (eds.) eBISS. LNBIP, vol. 138, pp. 29–61. Springer, Heidelberg (2013). https://doi.org/10.1007/978-3-642-36318-4_2
3. Indulska, M., Green, P., Recker, J., Rosemann, M.: Business process modeling: perceived benefits. In: Laender, A.H.F., Castano, S., Dayal, U., Casati, F., de Oliveira, J.P.M. (eds.) Conceptual Modeling - ER 2009, pp. 458–471. Springer, Heidelberg (2009)
4. Darai, D., Singh, S., Biswas, S.: Knowledge engineering-an overview. Int. J. Comput. Sci. Inf. Technol. 1(4), 230–234 (2010)
5. Kendal, S., Creen, M.: An Introduction to Knowledge Engineering. Springer, London (2007). https://doi.org/10.1007/978-1-84628-667-4
6. Sommerville, I.: Software Engineering. International Computer Science Series. Pearson, New York (2011)

7. Ganzha, M., Paprzycki, M., Pawłowski, W., Szmeja, P., Wasielewska, K.: Towards semantic interoperability between internet of things platforms. In: Gravina, R., Palau, C.E., Manso, M., Liotta, A., Fortino, G. (eds.) Integration, interconnection, and interoperability of IoT systems. IT, pp. 103–127. Springer, Cham (2018). https://doi.org/10.1007/978-3-319-61300-0_6

8. Friedrich, F., Mendling, J., Puhlmann, F.: Process model generation from natural language text. In: Mouratidis, H., Rolland, C. (eds.) CAiSE. LNCS, vol. 6741, pp. 482–496. Springer, Heidelberg (2011). https://doi.org/10.1007/978-3-642-21640-4_36

9. Kluza, K., Wiśniewski, P.: Spreadsheet-based business process modeling. In: 2016 Federated Conference on Computer Science and Information Systems (FedCSIS), pp. 1355–1358. IEEE (2016)

10. Kluza, K., Kagan, M., Wisniewski, P., Adrian, W.T., Ligeza, A.: Semantic-based support system for merging process knowledge from users. In: Mercier-Laurent, E., Owoc, M.L., Ritter, W. (eds.) AI4KM 2019: 7th International Workshop on Artificial Intelligence for Knowledge Management, Macao, China, 11 August 2019, pp. 56–61 (2019)

11. Wiśniewski, P., Kluza, K., Kucharska, E., Ligęza, A.: Spreadsheets as interoperability solution for business process representation. Appl. Sci. 9(2), 345 (2019)

12. Nalepa, G.J., Wojnicki, I.: Towards formalization of ARD+ conceptual design and refinement method. In: Wilson, D.C., Lane, H.C. (eds.) FLAIRS-21: Proceedings of the twenty-first international Florida Artificial Intelligence Research Society Conference, Coconut Grove, Florida, USA, 15–17 May 2008, pp. 353–358. AAAI Press, Menlo Park (2008)

13. Kluza, K., Wiśniewski, P., Adrian, W., Ligęza, A.: From attribute relationship diagrams to process (BPMN) and decision (DMN) models. In: Douligeris, C., Karagiannis, D., Apostolou, D. (eds.) KSEM 2019. LNCS (LNAI), vol. 11775, pp. 615–627. Springer, Cham (2019). https://doi.org/10.1007/978-3-030-29551-6_55

14. Shaw, M.L.G., Gaines, B.R.: Requirements acquisition. Softw. Eng. J. 11, 149–165 (1996)

15. Owoc, M.L., et al.: Benefits of knowledge acquisition systems for management. an empirical study. In: 2015 Federated Conference on Computer Science and Information Systems (FedCSIS), pp. 1691–1698. IEEE (2015)

16. Honkisz, K., Kluza, K., Wiśniewski, P.: A concept for generating business process models from natural language description. In: Liu, W., Giunchiglia, F., Yang, B. (eds.) KSEM 2018. LNCS (LNAI), vol. 11061, pp. 91–103. Springer, Cham (2018). https://doi.org/10.1007/978-3-319-99365-2_8

17. Welbank, M.: An overview of knowledge acquisition methods. Interact. Comput. 2(1), 83–91 (1990)

18. Olson, J.R., Rueter, H.H.: Extracting expertise from experts: methods for knowledge acquisition. Expert syst. 4(3), 152–168 (1987)

19. White, G.R., Cicmil, S.: Knowledge acquisition through process mapping. Int. J. Prod. Perf. Manage. (2016)

20. Silva, I., Sousa, P., Guerreiro, S.: Business processes compliance in partially observable environments. Technical report, EasyChair (2019)

21. La Rosa, M., Dumas, M., Ter Hofstede, A.H., Mendling, J.: Configurable multi-perspective business process models. Inf. Syst. 36(2), 313–340 (2011)

22. La Rosa, M., van der Aalst, W.M., Dumas, M., Ter Hofstede, A.H.: Questionnaire-based variability modeling for system configuration. Softw. Syst. Model. 8(2), 251–274 (2009)

23. Koschmider, A., Reijers, H.A.: Improving the process of process modelling by the use of domain process patterns. Enterpr. Inf. Syst. 9(1), 29–57 (2015)

24. Makni, L., Haddar, N.Z., Ben-Abdallah, H.: An automated method for the construction of semantic business process patterns. Int. J. Process Manage. Benchmark. 8(3), 263–290 (2018)

25. Fellmann, M., Delfmann, P., Koschmider, A., Laue, R., Leopold, H., Schoknecht, A.: Semantic technology in business process modeling and analysis. Part 2: domain patterns and (semantic) process model elicitation. In: EMISA Forum, vol. 35, pp. 12–23 (2015)

26. Koschmider, A., Hornung, T., Oberweis, A.: Recommendation-based editor for business process modeling. Data Knowl. Eng. **70**(6), 483–503 (2011)
27. Deng, S., et al.: A recommendation system to facilitate business process modeling. IEEE Trans. Cybern. **47**(6), 1380–1394 (2016)
28. Bobek, S., Baran, M., Kluza, K., Nalepa, G.J.: Application of bayesian networks to recommendations in business process modeling. In: AIBP@ AI* IA, pp. 41–50 (2013)
29. Mercier-Laurent, E.: Knowledge management & risk management. In: 2016 Federated Conference on Computer Science and Information Systems (FedCSIS), pp. 1369–1373. IEEE (2016)
30. van der Aalst, W.: Process Mining: Discovery, Conformance and Enhancement of Business Processes. Springer, Heidelberg (2011). https://doi.org/10.1007/978-3-642-19345-3
31. Ivanchikj, A., Pautasso, C.: Sketching process models by mining participant stories. In: Hildebrandt, T., van Dongen, B.F., Röglinger, M., Mendling, J. (eds.) BPM 2019. LNBIP, vol. 360, pp. 3–19. Springer, Cham (2019). https://doi.org/10.1007/978-3-030-26643-1_1
32. Riefer, M., Ternis, S.F., Thaler, T.: Mining process models from natural language text: a state-of-the-art analysis. Multikonferenz Wirtschaftsinformatik (MKWI 2016), pp. 9–11, March 2016
33. Sinha, A., Paradkar, A.: Use cases to process specifications in business process modeling notation. In: 2010 IEEE International Conference on Web Services, pp. 473–480. IEEE (2010)
34. de AR Goncalves, J.C., Santoro, F.M., Baiao, F.A.: Business process mining from group stories. In: 2009 13th International Conference on Computer Supported Cooperative Work in Design, pp. 161–166. IEEE (2009)
35. van der Aa, H., Di Ciccio, C., Leopold, H., Reijers, H.: Extracting declarative process models from natural language. In: Giorgini, P., Weber, B. (eds.) CAiSE. LNCS, vol. 11483, pp. 365–382. Springer, Cham (2019). https://doi.org/10.1007/978-3-030-21290-2_23
36. Kucharska, E., Grobler-Dębska, K., Klimek, R.: Collective decision making in dynamic vehicle routing problem. In: MATEC Web of Conferences, vol. 252, p. 03003. EDP Sciences (2019)
37. Nolte, A., Brown, R., Anslow, C., Wiechers, M., Polyvyanyy, A., Herrmann, T.: Collaborative business process modeling in multi-surface environments. In: Anslow, C., Campos, P., Jorge, J. (eds.) Collaboration Meets Interactive Spaces, pp. 259–286. Springer, Cham (2016). https://doi.org/10.1007/978-3-319-45853-3_12
38. Chounta, I.A., Nolte, A., Hecking, T., Farzan, R., Herrmann, T.: When to say "enough is enough!" a study on the evolution of collaboratively created process models. Proc. ACM Hum.-Comput. Interac. **1**(CSCW), 1–21 (2017)
39. Bird, S.: Nltk-lite: efficient scripting for natural language processing. In: Proceedings of the 4th International Conference on Natural Language Processing (ICON), pp. 11–18 (2005)
40. Wiśniewski, P., Kluza, K., Ligęza, A.: An approach to participatory business process modeling: BPMN model generation using Constraint Programming and graph composition. Appl. Sci. **8**(9), 1428 (2018)
41. Armas Cervantes, A., van Beest, N.R.T.P., La Rosa, M., Dumas, M., García-Bañuelos, L.: Interactive and incremental business process model repair. In: Panetto, H., et al. (eds.) OTM 2017. LNCS, vol. 10573, pp. 53–74. Springer, Cham (2017). https://doi.org/10.1007/978-3-319-69462-7_5
42. Adrian, W.T., Ligęza, A., Nalepa, G.J.: Inconsistency handling in collaborative knowledge management. In: 2013 Federated Conference on Computer Science and Information Systems, pp. 1233–1238. IEEE (2013)

The Concept of Crowdsourcing in Knowledge Management in Smart Cities

Łukasz Przysucha[✉]

Wroclaw University of Economics and Business,
Komandorska118/120 53-345, Wroclaw, Poland
lukasz.przysucha@ue.wroc.pl

Abstract. Crowdsourcing is a new approach and concept increasingly used in companies and organizations. Thanks to the outsourcing of tasks entrusted to the wider community, principals can obtain more detailed results and satisfactory results of outsourced activities. This idea has been considered so far in business terms, hardly anyone referred it to processes such as cities. The author presents in the article the idea of Smart City, the area of knowledge management and the use of Crowdsourcing processes for the freeing of communication channels between decision makers and residents. Crowdsourcing has been recognized in the field of public aspects, turning to the wider society. The author indicates an important gap in communication between the city's decision-makers and the inhabitants. In many agglomerations, city authorities do not have knowledge about the needs of residents, whereas the information cycle is disturbed. The main goal of the article is to build a flowchart/model of information flow using crowdsourcing and to discuss its place in intra-city communication.

Keywords: Crowdsourcing · Knowledge management · Smart City

1 Introduction

Our civilization is growing more and more. At the moment, people migrate from rural to urban areas around the world. Along with their movement, technology and available facilities and possibilities are developing. One should answer whether the current level of city management, communication between decision-makers and residents is adequate and whether it affects the development of the agglomeration. Do the metropolitan areas created have adequate grounds for further development and are able to avoid problems with functioning in the future? The author in the article analyzes the impact of crowdsourcing on improving communication in the city, and thus also the development of Smart City projects.

The article consists of 4 parts. The first one focuses on migration of people from rural to urban areas, impact on Smart City procedures and the need to take action in the area. The second part defines knowledge management processes in Smart City concepts, talking about the advantages and positive effects of the implementation of the knowledge

M. L. Owoc and M. Pondel (Eds.): AI4KM 2019, IFIP AICT 599, pp. 17–26, 2021.
https://doi.org/10.1007/978-3-030-85001-2_2

management idea. The next one is dedicated to crowdsourcing and its impact on knowledge management in the area of Smart City. The last part contains a diagram showing the idea of crowdsourcing in the area of knowledge management in Smart City.

2   The Development of the Smart City Idea

The idea of Smart City is a relatively new concept implemented and used by central and local authorities, economic entities and the city residents themselves. A smart city [1] is one that uses information and communication technologies (ICT) to increase the interactivity and efficiency of urban infrastructure and its components, as well as to raise the awareness of residents. Area of urban development and agglomeration is currently a strategic element of globalization and civilization in the world. The trend of settling urban areas on a global scale is more and more dynamic. In 1950, only 30% of the total population lived in cities, now it is almost 55%, while in 2050 it will be over 65% of the population [2] (attention should be paid to the global population increase). There are more and more mega cities with a population of over 10 million inhabitants. Currently, the most urbanized regions include North America (83% of residents living in cities in 2016), Latin America and the Caribbean (80%) and Europe (73%). Inhabitants of Africa and Asia live in most rural areas, at present 40% and 48% of their population live in urban areas. A continuous increase in the population of urban areas in the following decades is forecasted. Africa and Asia are urbanizing faster than other regions, and according to forecasts, by 2050, they will reach 56% and 64%, respectively, of urban living in the population. India, China and Nigeria are projected to jointly account for 37% of the forecast global urban population growth in 2014–2050. The estimated increase [3] of the population in urban areas in India is 404 million inhabitants, in China 292 million and Nigeria 212 million. Tokyo is currently the largest city in the world with an agglomeration of 38 million inhabitants, followed by Delhi with 25 million inhabitants and Shanghai with 23 million inhabitants. Mexico, Mumbai and São Paulo have a population of over 21 million. It is anticipated that by 2030, 41 megacities will be created around the world with over 10 million inhabitants. Forecasts indicate that Tokyo will remain the largest city in the world in 2030, with 37 million inhabitants, followed by Delhi, where the population is expected to grow rapidly to 36 million [4].

The development of urban agglomerations has many positive aspects for our civilization, but it is accompanied by many problems. The main one focuses on proper city management.

The concept of smart city, depending on the various definitions and scopes can include many aspects of life. According to this basic smart city can be called the area (city, region, agglomeration), which consists of four elements [5]. The first of these are creative residents who are "enlightened" their activities and use their knowledge as well as develop it. Another pillar is effectively working organizations and institutions processing existing knowledge [6]. On the technical side must be ensured adequate technological infrastructure broadband cable services in the network, digital space for data and remote tools for knowledge management. The final element is the ability to innovation. Komninos N. explains this as part of management and the ability to solve problems that appear for the first time since the innovation and management under uncertainty are key to assessing intelligence (Table 1).

Table 1. Benefits and threats in the Smart City model.

Comparison	
Benefits	*Threats*
Smart Cities help people to live, work and play with others while requiring fewer resources	Lack of electricity causes paralysis
It helps in controlling water, environment and conservation of animal populations	There are concerns about data privacy and security
It reduces traffic jams	Cities find it difficult to work across departments and boundaries
Facilitates access to the doctor	Addicted to the use of electronic equipment
Fast reaction time in case of danger	The ability to manipulate the target messages by the municipal authorities

In the process of creating Smart City, it is extremely important to create a structured resource of current (and updated) data that will be used by the administration and at the same time will be made available to residents to help them deal with official matters and, on the other, to get to know the city.

Under the influence of globalization, Smart City definitions change their dimensions in terms of time and space. They can be enclosed in three dimensions global space covering a set of cities, on a lower level there is a local space corresponding to a city located in a given geographical area and another area of influence covering the field of interaction of the city with other cities.

The author has conducted research among residents of the city of Wroclaw in Poland, in terms of what residents associate the concept of Smart City. The study was conducted among 200 city residents, taking into account the differentiation in sex, age and work performed. The survey was conducted in December 2018 in paper form in Polish (Fig. 1).

It should be noted that a very large number of respondents replied that the concept of Smart City is associated with new technologies and easy, simplified communication with decision makers in the city. As many as 54% of those surveyed associate Smart City with new technologies. In additional dialogs, they marked mainly communication devices such as social networks, thought exchange places, applications and tools supporting Smart Society.

An equally popular association, as many as 41% of respondents answered that there is easy contact with the city administration. At this point, the residents commented on the possibility of influencing the processes in the city, co-deciding about projects and

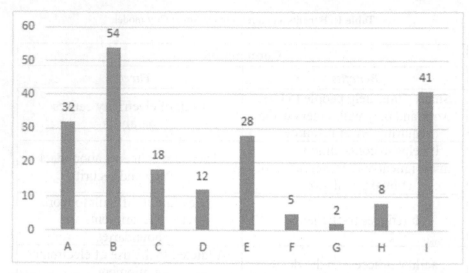

Fig. 1. Associations regarding Smart City. Chart legend: A - Intelligent public transport. B - New tele information systems. C - Fast Internet. D - Professional health service. E - Clean air and renewable energy sources. F - Social ties. G - Exchange of knowledge. H - Facilitation in shopping. I - Easy contact with the city administration

development of the city, awareness of creating their own image among the Smart Society and belonging to the community that develops and creates activities in the area.

3   Knowledge Management in the Smart City Area

One of the best-known definitions for knowledge management is the one that defines them as the process of creating, sharing, modifying and using information and knowledge in a given area [7]. It is often heard that knowledge management is an element of organizations or companies. However, this is one of the areas where these processes and rules can be found. The implementation of knowledge management within cities has become very popular recently. Using the resident portals, i.e. electronic sites enabling them to connect to a given server, residents are able to retrieve knowledge and data that are transmitted in real time by institutions or exchange of information between them. Looking at the urban agglomeration, one should look in many ways for a company. The main goal, however, will be the well-being of the citizen and his security, comfort of living, speed of dealing with various matters, education, etc.

However, city management is very similar to the company management, because the authorities get a specific budget, they have specific goals and possibilities to achieve. In this case, also management processes will often be similar to those in organizations and business.

Below is a chart showing the expectations of the inhabitants of Wroclaw, Poland in the field of knowledge management in the Smart City area. As in the previous survey, 200 respondents were included (Fig. 2).

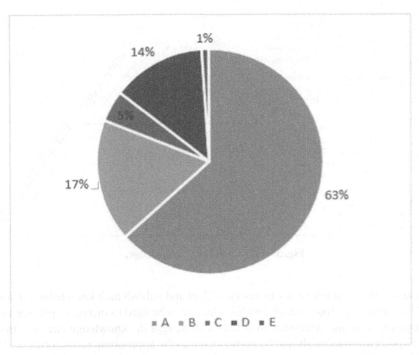

Fig. 2. Expectations of residents in the field of knowledge management in the urban area. Chart legend: A - On-line portal for knowledge exchange within the city. B - Events and meetings dedicated thematically for individual groups of residents. C - Stationary places, allowing coming and acquiring general knowledge, interdisciplenary. D - Knowledge base as a material value for the city and its future generations. E - Exchange of knowledge with other unconventional media such as local newspapers and radio

The survey shows that residents expect mainly interactive knowledge sharing tools, accessible through ICT resources such as social media or the Internet. As many as 63% of the respondents indicated that they lacked a portal for local interaction between users. In the replies, it can also find comments that the portal should be available in real mode both via the Internet stationary as well as mobile. The next places are occupied by elements widgets, applications and all kinds of possibilities to organize meetings between residents with similar interests, hobbies and professions.

It should be noted that residents must be made aware of the importance of the Smart City concept and know what benefits it brings (Fig. 3). In the field of Knowledge Management, two types of knowledge can be distinguished [8].

Tacit knowledge and explicit knowledge. As in organizations and businesses, residents also aggregate and exchange knowledge. In connection with this, when analyzing information flows in agglomerations, one can come to the conclusion that there is also both tacit and explicit knowledge in urban areas. Tacit knowledge is existing only in the mind of the man who owns it, created as a result of experience and not fully conscious ("I know that I can do it"), manifested only through skillful action. Explicit knowledge, however, is expressed in a character form and is written on the carriers of knowledge. In

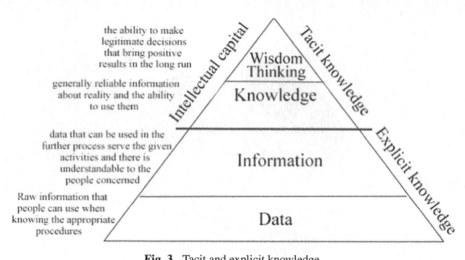

Fig. 3. Tacit and explicit knowledge.

the case of cities, it is necessary to verify, collect and publish tacit knowledge for wider use. This knowledge base, which residents have, can be used to increase agglomeration development. It is also necessary to collect and manage the knowledge already discovered. Explicit knowledge should be segregated into the appropriate repositories, and the proper algorithms, instructions and operating diagrams may indicate the possibilities of using it.

Many scientists analyze the role of Knowledge Management in Smart City. For example, Negre, E., Rosenthal-Sabroux, C., & Gascó, M. propose [9] a novel and innovative Smart City concept based on people's information and knowledge, which aims to improve decision-making processes and add value to the business processes of a modern city. Other authors, Nam, T., and Pardo, T. A. identify [10] the components underlying the Smart City concept and key factors of the successful Smart City initiative.

4 Crowdsourcing and Its Influence on Knowledge Management in Smart City Processes

The subject of crowdsourcing is quite a new, yet undiscovered, research area. Analyzing literature, we can only find a few books on the market that are devoted to crowdsourcing used commercially on the market. There is still a research gap in the use of crowdsourcing at the level of urban communities. Literature in the subject matter focuses mainly on scientific articles, the intensification of which can be attributed to the years 2018 and 2019 [11].

Crowdsourcing is a process [12] that uses the wisdom and potential of the community for the purpose of the individual or for the public good. It involves the outsourcing of a given task to the crowd, i.e. an unspecified number of random people. Crowdsourcing owes its rapid development to the Internet tool, i.e. the site that gathers millions of Internet users from all over the world, enabling all of them to participate in the tasks that were once reserved for a narrow group of specialists. Crowdsourcing are elements that can take different forms, depending on the conditions, their final purpose and use. It can be aimed at acquiring and generating new, creative ideas. Thanks to crowdsourcing, city authorities can create new solutions that will be conducive to the local community. Another use may be to give feedback on specific queries. This is the process of collecting user feedback on Smart City project data. Crowdsourcing can develop knowledge management processes in relation to Smart City projects. Acquiring knowledge from the crowd gives more opportunities, diversity of data and better exchange of information between residents and decision-makers. This, in turn, results in the awareness of the effectiveness of action, the sense of sharing knowledge and increasing motivation to engage in the process.

5 Model of Distribution of Knowledge Between Residents and Decision Makers

Crowdsourcing in the area of Smart City means first and foremost the use of knowledge of residents by decision makers and the government. At this stage, one should ask the question what factors determine the involvement of stakeholders in acquiring knowledge. How can we influence their motivation and willingness to share information and knowledge? From the technical point of view, the question is also what tools are used to acquire knowledge from target stakeholders and to what extent can the acquired knowledge be used in Smart City projects? In cities there are information gaps at the communication level between decision-makers and residents. It is also important how we can supplement our information resources to reduce the information gap.

The main questions for residents (people who have knowledge that can be used in the crowdsourcing process), but also city decision makers are:

A. *Under what terms and when you would like to share your resources?*
B. *What internal and external factors influence your motivation to share knowledge*
C. *Are Social Media and Resident Portal appropriate information channels?*
D. *What do you think about building a local social image? Are you willing to participate publicly in the future in the debate about your region and represent others?*
E. *What do you think about building a local social image? Are you willing to participate publicly in the future in the debate about your region and represent others?*
F. *Do you want to co-decide about urban processes?*

Crowdsourcing as a process can have many advantages resulting from its implementation in given places. These can be corporations, organizations, as well as urban agglomerations and other clusters of people who can support the processes of acquiring and transferring knowledge.

The main advantages of crowdsourcing in relation to the urban community may include [13]:

A. *Saving time and money.*
The crowd generates ideas much faster and the preparation of the website is definitely cheaper than paying for the work of a narrow, specialized team.

B. *The variety of submitted projects and their originality.*
Many perspectives and points of view. As with the development of GNU GPL applications available to thousands of users, many programmers have many points of view, which means that the systems are very diverse and have thousands of additions, templates and widgets. In the case of acquiring knowledge from the crowd using crowdsourcing, this process looks similar.

C. *Obtaining information on the needs and expectations of residents.*
The process of exchanging messages and needs between residents and decisionmakers in a given location is extremely important because it develops Smart Society, the residents feel understood and have a real influence on deciding on important issues in the area of the immediate environment. The rulers are not detached from reality and their opinion is compatible with the rest of the people living in the agglomeration.

D. *Creating a committed community.*
An engaged community can greatly influence positive changes in the city. Thanks to the awareness and commitment of people, the government can develop all areas of Smart City. Residents and the government (with extensive experience) can create Collective Intelligence.

E. *Marketing and promotional benefits.*
Using crowdsourcing can also be a positive urban element, which will be made available to other municipal units. This can be treated as a marketing element of the urban strategy.

Below, the author presents a general knowledge distribution scheme in the area of Smart City, including Task Crowdsourcing (Fig. 4).

It should be understood that Crowdsourcing is a response to the lack of knowledge demand. It forces the process of knowledge acquisition, which is carried out by the crowdsourcing process. Crowdsourcing triggers engagement in target users (in the case of Smart City residents). It is directly related to the motivation that makes the willingness to share knowledge between residents and the government. This process is dual and returnable. Commitment, in turn, develops the knowledge of the residents.

This in turn with the knowledge of the rulers (who have the appropriate experience) creates collective intelligence. Crowdsourcing is a form of collective intelligence. It can be done through modern ICT tools. These tools generate applications, constitute social media via the Internet.

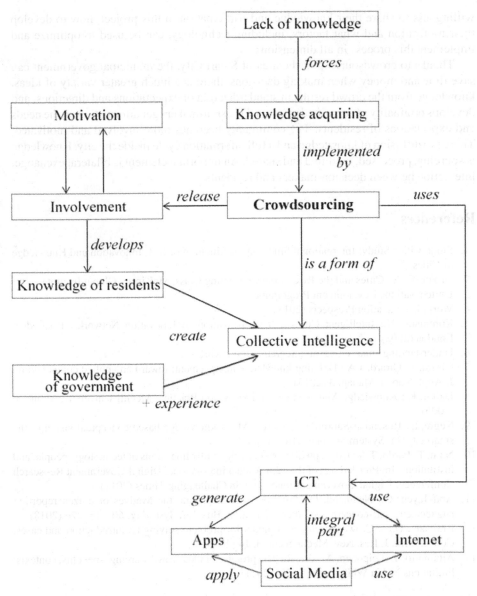

Fig. 4. General knowledge distribution scheme in the area of Smart City.

6   Conclusion

Crowdsourcing as a process occurs in many places. So far, most of the definitions were based on organizations and companies. In the last 2–3 years, he began to appear in relation to Smart City. Using Crowdsourcing to acquire knowledge from residents can help exchange knowledge between residents, decision makers and the government. However, one should ask yourself what factors can affect the involvement of residents in the willingness to share their knowledge and participation in this project, how to develop their motivation and what factors, including technology, can be used to optimize and implement this process in all dimensions.

Thanks to crowdsourcing in the area of Smart City, the municipal government can save time and money when making decisions, there is a much greater variety of ideas, knowledge from the crowd results in standardization of expectations and directions, and develops originality of submitted projects. Decision-makers get information on the needs and expectations of residents. The community becomes more involved and motivated. There is a diffusion of knowledge and a full information cycle inside the city. Knowledge is sourcing, processed, modified and shared. An important element is bilateral exchange, interaction between decision-makers and residents.

References

1. Smart Cities Study: International Study on the Situation of ICT, Innovation and Knowledge in Cities.
2. Urban World: Cities and the Rise of the Consuming Class, McKinsey Global Institute
3. United Nations Development Programme
4. World Urbanization Prospects (2018)
5. Komninos, N.: Intelligent Cities and Globalization of Innovation Networks, Routledge, London (2008)
6. Understanding smart cities: an integrative framework
7. Girard, J., Girard, J.A.: Defining knowledge management: toward an applied compendium. J. Appl. Knowl. Manag. **3** (2015)
8. Dalkir, K.: Knowledge Management in Theory and Practice, McGill University, Montréal (2005)
9. Negre, E., Rosenthal-Sabroux, C., Gascó, M.: A knowledge-based conceptual vision of the smart city. In: System Sciences HICSS (2015)
10. Nam, T., Pardo, T.A.: Conceptualizing smart city with dimensions of technology, people, and institutions. In: Proceedings of the 12th Annual International Digital Government Re- search Conference: Digital Government Innovation in Challenging Times (2011)
11. Abu-Tayeh, G., Neumann, O., Stuermer, M.: Exploring the Motives of citizen reporting engagement: self-concern and other-orientation, Bus. Inf. Syst. Eng. **60**, 215–226 (2018)
12. Brabham, D.C.: Crowdsourcing as a model for problem solving an introduction and cases. Converg. Int. J. Res. New Media Technol. **14** (2008)
13. Aitamurto, T., Leiponen, A., Tee, R.: The promise of idea crowdsourcing – benefits, contexts, limitations Nokia White Paper **1** (30) (2011)

The Impact of Big Data on Smart City Concepts

Anna Reklewska[✉]

Wroclaw University of Economics and Business,
Komandorska 118/120, 53-345 Wroclaw, Poland

Abstract. The main aim of the paper is to analyse the possibilities of using big data as a part of a smart city and indicate what challenges cities face during big data analytics implementation. The author divided this paper into three, main sections. In the first part, the author has described a concept of smart city, explaining why this concept has become so important and popular in recent years. In the second part of the article, the author has presented the concept of big data, giving the definition, the most important characteristics and general examples allowing a better understanding of this field. Finally, in a key part of the paper, these two concepts have been combined together to indicate fields they should complement each other to positively influence the cities' development and achieving its goals. In the last part of the article, the author gave examples of benefits that cities can see in the implementation of the big data analysis, as well as examples of big data projects combined with the cities in which they have been implemented. Results of a paper show that nowadays, the implementation of big data technology may have a positive impact on smart city development.

Keywords: Smart city · Smart technology · Big data · ICT · Knowledge management · Artificial intelligence

1 Introduction

Cities generate huge amounts of raw data every day. Date are produced by people, applications, systems and much more. The correct collection and use of this data can be extremely beneficial to cities. At the same time for several years we have seen higher interest of the concept of smart cities. We hear and read about cities that are even surpassing themselves in being smarter, doing so on the one hand to benefit and make amenities for their citizens and on the other hand to tackle the growing problems of urbanisation, climate change and so on. The author of this paper decided to bring together two concepts: big data and smart city, and to present what a combination of them can result. The main aim of this paper is to present the potential benefits of using big data in modern cities, as well as to indicate what challenges can cities face trying to implement solutions related to big data applications. In the first part of this paper, the author focused on the concept of smart city, explaining its definitions and describing the components, in order to present how many data sources are in modern cities. In the following chapter, the author describes the concept of big data explaining how to effectively use the collected

© IFIP International Federation for Information Processing 2021
Published by Springer Nature Switzerland AG 2021
M. L. Owoc and M. Pondel (Eds.): AI4KM 2019, IFIP AICT 599, pp. 27–36, 2021.
https://doi.org/10.1007/978-3-030-85001-2_3

data and giving important characteristics. In the last part of the paper, the author focuses on both concepts, showing the benefits of their combination and examples of solutions already functioning today. The last part of a paper is about results of using big data solutions in smart cities.

2 Smart City Characteristics

Cities are an increasingly important element of civilization. According to the statistics of United Nations (UN), by 2050, around 68% of the world's population will be living in urban areas. The gradual shift in residence of the human population to urban areas, combined with the growth of the world's population could add about 2.5 billion people to urban areas by 2050. [1] The current number of city dwellers, especially in the largest cities, as well as a perspective of the continued growth of this population, makes the recourses of the cities limited. City government faces new, previously unknown challenges. The problems of the cities can be divided into the following categories: social, economic and organisational. Examples of these problems include communication and transport problems, environmental pollution and ecology or adaptation urban space to modern needs of city dwellers. [2] In literature, urban development concept based on modern technologies and innovative way of managing the city is named smart city. In research and scientific sources, there is not any single appropriate definition of this term as so it can be interpreted in many ways. One of the definitions is that "a smart city is (…) a city which invests in ICT enhanced governance enhanced governance and participatory processes to define appropriate public service and transportation investments that can ensure sustainable socio- economic development, enhanced quality-of-life, and intelligent management of natural resources" [3], however by another definition smart city is "a well performing in a forward-looking way in economy, people, governance, mobility, environment and living, built on the smart combination of endowments and activities of self-decisive, independent and aware citizens." [4] It is necessary to consider what characteristics a city must have in order to be called a smart city. The table below shows the components of smart city along with their description.

Table 1. Components of smart city.

Components	Description
Smart economy	Means using Information and Communication Technologies (ICT) for business. A smart economy can also mean better flow of information and knowledge, as well as goods and services
Smart mobility	Means innovative transport and logistics systems, using ICT to enable the safe and efficient movement of people and goods They can also be used to collect data on the current transport situation and its subsequent use, e.g. for a traffic management
Smart environment	Means solutions for controlling emissions and energy consumption In this area, Information and Communication Technologies can be used for street and building lighting or waste management

(*continued*)

Table 1. (*continued*)

Components	Description
Smart people	Means an appropriate level of education. Smart people are city dwellers who use various intelligent solutions in their everyday activities, both in their private and professional lives
Smart living	This component is similar to smart people. Smart living means that smart city dwellers use modern technologies every day. Smart living refers, among other things, to concepts such as smart homes and smart workplaces
Smart governance	Means intelligent management of public administration, i.e. integrated management of all subsystems of a city. City dwellers, public benefit organizations and private companies should also participate in the management of these systems

Table 1 does not indicate all areas of city management that are components of smart cities. In order to better understand the topic of smart cities, three groups of factors that make up a smart city can be identified [5]:

- Technology factors,
- Institutional factors,
- Human factors.

The first of them, technology factors, are digital solutions that improve the functioning of the city's subsystems. The next of them, institutional factors, concern activities carried out by city administrations and politicians. This factor includes all legal acts, regulations, and institutions, whose task is to support the development of smart cities. Third, human factor, includes an educated society that is willing to use new technologies and responsive to changes (Fig. 1).

An essential element of smart city is knowledge. However, before we can gain access to knowledge, we need to analyze the sources of data that allow us to obtain it. Examples of such sources include [6]:

- data from public registers: population register, real estate register, business activity register etc.
- local development plans,
- database of topographical objects,
- data from waste management systems, paid parking zones, cultural institutions,
- data collected by various sensors and sensors monitoring infrastructure and the urban environment, e.g. in the field of energy: air and water quality, traffic volume,
- crowdsourcing - data obtained directly from residents and communities,
- data made available by city dwellers using social media applications e.g. applications for monitoring physical activity,
- aerial and satellite images,

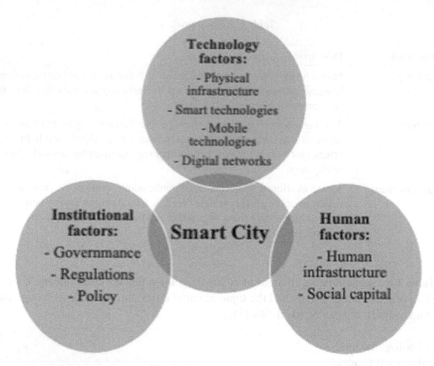

Fig. 1. Factors of smart city.

- financial data, including local taxes and charges
- data collected by companies for their operations, which can be used by cities, e.g. data from mobile operators.

3   Big Data Assumptions

Today and every day, people collect, analyze and store huge amount of data. From a historical perspective, big data is not something totally new. Data was already stored in data warehouses in the 1990s, but they were not as extensive as they are now. So what does big data mean nowadays? Watson characterize big data as having:

- High volume – the amount or quantity of data,
- High velocity – the rate at which data is created,
- High variety – the different types of data. [7]

In the extended version of this definition, Watson explains that "Big data is a term that is used to describe data that is high volume, high velocity, and/or high variety; requires new technologies and techniques to capture, store, and analyze it; and is used to enhance decision making, provide insight and discovery, and support and optimize processes".

Big data is characterized by the following methods of information analysis:

- possibility of analyzing very large data sets,
- ability to analyze disordered data,
- the searching for relations between effects and causes.

The characteristics described above indicate that big data analyses differ from classical information analyzes. In big data analyses, any data set, even the smallest one, can be of great importance. With the use of big data technology, the decision- making process, based on bug data sets is supported, and many people, both from the world of science and business, see this potential, not only in the storage of information but, what is more important, in its analysis.

There are many sources of big data. Examples of data sources are shown in Fig. 2.

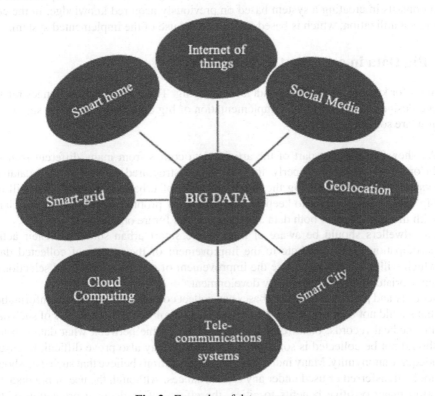

Fig. 2. Examples of data sources.

The process of building useful data using big data analyzes can be divided into the following parts [8]:

- Data creation,
- Collecting data,

- Creating ideas,
- Processed data,
- Inference,
- Implementation,
- Utilization.

The first of these stages concerns the creation of data by various sources. They can be produced consciously or only accompany specific phenomena. The next stage, that is data collection, may take place in various ways. Information may be collected voluntarily or compulsorily, some of them spontaneously, and others according to a specific key. The next stage is creating the idea. Based on it, a data analysis algorithm will be created from a specific source. Its result is a data processing step, the aim of which is to develop a model of a given phenomenon. Inference is the stage of extracting knowledge from the information collected, and the transfer of this knowledge to real use is an implementation that consists in creating a system based on previously acquired knowledge. In the end, there is a utilization, which is based on the current use of the implemented system.

4 Big Data in a Context of Smart City

Mining for knowledge from big data is challenging. There are many challenges related to the design, development and implementation of big data applications for smart city. Below are some of them [9]:

- As shown in the first part of the article, data comes from many different sources. In order to use them properly, they should be structured using advanced database systems. When considering the implementation of urban applications that will use big data, it is important to keep in mind the many problems that may be associated with this and relate to both data collection and its future organisation.
- city dwellers should be aware of how to use smart urban solutions. Their active participation may contribute to the improvement of the quality of collected data, which will positively influence the improvement of the functioning and selection of appropriate directions of the city development.
- security and privacy issues. Databases can collect confidential and private information that should not be processed or require a high level of security. Examples of such data are medical records, bank records, etc. The borderline between what data can and should not be collected is sometimes very thin. It may also prove difficult to ensure adequate anonymity. Many individuals and organisations believe that such data should not be transferred or used under any circumstances. Although the use of big data can bring many positive benefits to cities, the effects of inadequate protection of the information collected can be irreversible and disastrous.

These challenges have different impacts on the performance of smart city applications and create different levels of difficulty. Moreover, different applications have different requirements for data usage.

Data, generated from multiple sources, can be catalogued and stored in different locations, owned by different actors. There are many opportunities to use big data to solve problems, through data analysis, data intelligence and data mining. To facilitate this huge demand for resources to support big data analysis, the Cloud was used. The Cloud is a suitable platform for applications with a high demand for resources, enabling active cooperation between different applications. Through the use of cloud computing, cities have gained access to a huge amount of computing power.

"Currently, many cities compete to be smart cities in hopes of reaping some of their benefits economically, environmentally and socially". Examples of benefits of transforming a city into a smart city include:

- Efficient resource utilization: at a time when resources are shrinking at a very rapid rate, it is essential to know how to allocate available resources so that their consumption is as low as possible. "In addition, one of the important aspects of smart city applications is that they are designed for interconnectivity and data collections which can also facilitate better collaboration across applications and services."
- better quality of life: primarily the result of better urban areas planning, more efficient and city dwellers-friendly transport systems and better and faster services.
- better access to information: this benefit makes access to information easier for all city-dwellers and the share of knowledge will become obvious.

These and other benefits can only be achieved if cities invest in more technology and the successful use of big data analysis. Innovation technology can be very useful when considering city resource management and decision making.

Implementation of big data application in smart cities requires a lot of support from information and communication technology (ICT). This technology provides ways to solve many of the problems that smart cities face. There are many examples indicating that the role of big data in smart city is very important. Some of them are indicated below:

- Smart education: analysis of big data has an impact on education, increasing the efficiency and productivity of education processes using smart education services. Smart education applications can engage people in an active learning environment. By analyzing big data education institutions can control whether they are using their resources properly.
- Smart grid [10]: electricity delivery system, which effectively responds to the behavior of all connected entities (generator, customer/prosumer, network operator), integrated with information and communication technology, enhanced grid operations, customer services, and environmental benefits. Smart grid continuously controls what happens at different stages of the energy flow, allowing the possibility of controlling this process.
- Smart healthcare [11]: the application of big data analytics in healthcare has a lot of positive outcomes. Big data refers to huge amounts of information that are consolidated and analyzed by specific technologies. When used in healthcare, they will use specific data on the health status of a population or individual and help to treat diseases, reduce costs or prevent epidemics.

According to the Smart City Maturity Model proposed by IDC Government Insights [12], we can identify five stages of a smart city maturity: Ad hoc, Opportunistic, Repeatable, Managed, Optimized. In the context of the use of data generated in the city, this classification may be as follows:

- Ad hoc stage: In cities at the lowest level, data use and integration are limited. Data is used primarily to provide a specific service. There may be issues related to data integrity quality, security and privacy
- Opportunistic stage: At this level we can see the first attempts at advanced data analysis, there are single applications for this analysis. The data may be published for use by other entities.
- Repeatable stage: On the third level, cities consciously use data. They invest in advanced data management, data collection, analysis and big data applications. A wide range of open data is published with the strategic intention to use it to stimulate innovation. City dwellers create and share data in key areas.
- Managed stage: The next level is a fully managed system. Cities use extended data collection and analysis that leads to better decision making and service design. City dwellers are aware of the benefits of data analysis and are willing to engage in new initiatives.
- Optimized stage: The most developed cities in the world are on the last level. Many big data applications are created. They use data analytics to dynamically, automatically predict and preventively improve their services. It is possible to react in real time.

In this section, some of the example use cases of big-data analytics in a smart-city context are presented. These examples can serve as inspiration for creating solutions using big data analysis to improve the quality of life of big city dwellers. As we can see below big data analyzes are helping cities around the world (Table 2):

Table 2. Big data projects in smart cities.

Smart city component	Big data projects	Location
Smart transport	The city of Nanjing, China, has installed sensors in taxis, buses and one million private cars. The data is transmitted daily to the Nanjing Information Center, where experts are able to analyze traffic data and traffic locations and peak times to then send updates to commuters on their smartphones. With this information, government officials have created new traffic routes by avoiding traffic jams and suggesting the best routes at the moment without spending money on new roads. [13]	Nanjing, China

(*continued*)

Table 2. (*continued*)

Smart city component	Big data projects	Location
Smart transport, smart living	The main Italian railway operator has installed sensors in all its trains and now receives real-time updates of the mechanical condition of each train and forecasts for future repairs and maintenance. This data makes it possible to plan actions before trains fail, which would cause many problems for travelers. These technological innovations provide passengers with a reliable system and services, while avoiding major disruptions to cities	Italy
Smart living, smart people	Wroclaw, Poland has introduced a system in which city dwellers can submit their ideas for using the city budget. The administrators of this system collect all the submitted ideas, both those implemented and those rejected, creating a database of the greatest needs of the residents. Based on these data, projects and improvements are implemented in the city, as well as repair works. The ideas gathered in the system concern education, infrastructure, culture and many others	Wroclaw, Poland (and many others polish cities)
Smart living, smart mobility	The project created by several universities combined data from mobile phone networks, traffic monitoring systems and vehicle tracking systems. In addition to providing information on the situation on the roads and traffic, it allows to plan the city's infrastructure by analysing the collected data. The application is also used for mass events	Czech Republic
Smart transport, smart mobility	In Amsterdam, almost all car parks are managed digitally using an application. Anyone who wants to book a parking space enters their vehicle registration number. The digital platform connected to the application recognizes	Amsterdam, Rotterdam, The Netherlands
	the vehicle In Rotterdam, sensors are installed to guide the drivers to free spaces	
Smart environment	Los Angeles is replacing traditional streetlights with the new LEDs. The new lights will be an interconnected system that will inform the city administration of each bulb's status. If one malfunctions, it can be identified and fixed immediately	Los Angeles, United States

In conclusion, it would be appropriate to reconsider the issues that should be addressed in future studies. Many of them are the result of the previously presented examples of using big data in smart city. The most important are data security, privacy and information protection. Another important issue is also the growing need for highly educated people who will be able to design and operate intelligent platforms and applications operating from the city. Another need is to establish common rules for the control of intelligent solutions in the city. In a smart city it is required to monitor and control initiatives and implementations using various tools and techniques to ensure the correctness, effectiveness and quality of the implemented applications. All these needs should be taken into account when analyzing the use of big data in smart city.

5   Conclusion

The article presents a role of big data in smart cities. Both smart city and big data are two modern and increasingly popular concepts in recent years. The article presents the potential of using big data in smart city development. Combining these two concepts and building intelligent urban applications can positively affect the achievement of a better quality of life for residents and intelligent management of urban resources. Progress in the field of big data has enabled cities to access information that has never been available before, and a well-developed strategy for data analysis gives cities the opportunity to access extremely important knowledge and easily gain significant, practical insights. When a city can monitor desired indicators in real time, the level of its innovation can quickly increase. Big data offers endless possibilities to make better decisions. Building and implementing smart cities based on big data will require challenges and open issues, the use of professional design and development models, well-trained human resources, and being prepared and well supported by management units. With all success factors and a better understanding of the concept, making a smart city will be possible, and a further improvement in smarter solutions will be realizable. The ability to collect and use city data is what makes city smart.

References

1. https://www.un.org/development/desa/publications/2018-revision-of-world-urbanization-prospects.html
2. Przysucha, L.: Knowledge management processes in smart city-electronic tools supporting the exchange of information and knowledge among city residents. Int. J. Innov. Manag. Technol. 10(4), 155–160 (2019)
3. Khan, Z., Anjum, A., Kiani, S.L.: Cloud based big data analytics for smart future cities. In: Proceedings of the 2013 IEEE/ACM 6th International Conference on Utility and Cloud Computing. IEEE Computer Society (2013)
4. Giffinger, R., Fertner, C., Kramar, H., Kalasek, R., Pichler-Milanovic, N., Meijers, E.: Smart Cities: Ranking of European Medium-sized Cities (2007)
5. Nam, T., Pardo, T., Conceptualizing smart city with dimensions of technology, people, and institutions. In: The Proceedings of the 12th Annual International Conference on Digital Government Research (2013)
6. http://smartcity-expert.eu/
7. Watson, H.: Tutorial: Big Data Analytics: Concepts, Technologies, and Applications. Communications of the Association for Information Systems (2014)
8. Jasińska, K.: Big Data – wielkie perspektywy i wielkie problem (2015)
9. Nader, M., Al-Jaroodi, J., et al.: Applications of big data to smart city (2015)
10. Shabanzadeh, M., Parsa Moghaddam, M.: What is the Smart Grid? (2014)
11. https://www.datapine.com/blog/big-data-examples-in-healthcare/
12. https://www.innovations.harvard.edu/idc-releases-first-smart-city-maturity-model
13. Gonfalonieri, A.: Big Data & Smart Cities: How can we prepare for them? (2018)

Artificial Intelligence Technologies in Education: Benefits, Challenges and Strategies of Implementation

Mieczysław L. Owoc[1]([⊠]) [iD], Agnieszka Sawicka[1] [iD], and Paweł Weichbroth[2] [iD]

[1] Wrocław University of Economics and Business, Komandorska 118/120 street,
53-345 Wrocław, Poland
{mieczyslaw.owoc,agnieszka.sawicka}@ue.wroc.pl
[2] Faculty of Electronics, Telecommunications and Informatics, Department of Software
Engineering, Gdańsk University of Technology, 11/12 Gabriela Narutowicza Street,
80-233 Gdańsk, Poland
pawel.weichbroth@pg.edu.pl
http://www.ue.wroc.pl/en/, https://pg.edu.pl/en/home

Abstract. Since the education sector is associated with highly dynamic business environments which are controlled and maintained by information systems, recent technological advancements and the increasing pace of adopting artificial intelligence (AI) technologies constitute a need to identify and analyze the issues regarding their implementation in education sector. However, a study of the contemporary literature reveled that relatively little research has been undertaken in this area. To fill this void, we have identified the benefits and challenges of implementing artificial intelligence in the education sector, preceded by a short discussion on the concepts of AI and its evolution over time. Moreover, we have also reviewed modern AI technologies for learners and educators, currently available on the software market, evaluating their usefulness. Last but not least, we have developed a strategy implementation model, described by a five-stage, generic process, along with the corresponding configuration guide. To verify and validate their design, we separately developed three implementation strategies for three different higher education organizations. We believe that the obtained results will contribute to better understanding the specificities of AI systems, services and tools, and afterwards pave a smooth way in their implementation.

Keywords: Artificial intelligence · Benefit · Challenge · Strategy · Implementation

1 Introduction

Research into artificial intelligence (AI) has tended to increase for a number of reasons. The desire and excitement to create intelligent systems was the case in the past in the academic community, while now it seems inevitable that their development and inception have been addressed by the majority of organizations, representing almost all business sectors. It is not only the effect of the far-reaching technological progress such as microprocessors, data storage and global networking, but also the impact of changes in business strategies. While the debate on how AI will change business is at the top of the present-day agenda [1], education is already being challenged to reconceptualize existing teaching and learning methods by putting AI techniques and tools into service [2–4].

Indeed, Sameer Maskey, founder and CEO at Fusemachines, an AI Education and AI Talent Solution provider based in New York City (USA), in an interview with Forbes magazine published on 8th June 2020, said that [5]: "It will be important for educators and policymakers to explore the intersection of education and artificial intelligence. The application of machines in learning environments is only one variable in a multifaceted equation. We have to consider barriers that prevent an even distribution in technological resources and how to overcome them. We must also ensure that teachers are prepared and empowered to leverage artificial intelligence. Assuming these elements are addressed, the possibilities of AI-powered learning are infinite".

Inspired by his words, and apart from the financial costs and profits, the question arises what are the specific benefits and challenges of implementing artificial intelligence in education? Since little work has focused on this area, the first research goal is to identify and analyze its possible benefits and preceding challenges (see Sects. 2.2 and 2.3, respectively). In this case, a qualitative generic thematic analysis was undertaken due to its flexibility to collect descriptive data in the narrative form.

Our study is also driven by a concern for the implications of the human factor due to the increasing evidence of the apprehension raised against the proliferation of artificial intelligence since the variety of its applications seems to be immeasurable, ranging from computer games [6, 7], decision-making [8–10], education [11–16], enterprise management [17–19], grid computing [20–23], knowledge management [24–27], learning systems [28–31], ontologies [32–34], smart cities [35–37], and software engineering [38–40], to name just a few. On the contrary, we attempt to argue that AI can amplify educational effectiveness, concerned with sharing, developing and disseminating knowledge, at the same time preserving human autonomy, agency and capabilities. Therefore, the second research goal is to analyze and evaluate the usefulness of existing AI technologies (see Sect. 2.4).

To explore these two goals, we collect, analyze and review a plethora of information sources. Their addresses were obtained from the Google web search engine and Google Scholar website by using combinations of keywords such as: "artificial intelligence", "adoption", "acceptance", "advantages", "disadvantages", "implementation", "deployment", "education", "benefits", "challenges", "risks", and "technologies".

What is much rarer, however, was to find applicable and relevant implementation strategies. Nevertheless, based on our previous results, which provide solid theoretical foundation, we also designed and created a generic strategy, able to be applied in a strategic plan regarding any of the AI systems, services or tools in all industries, and in organizations of a variety of sizes. In particular, our strategy addresses the "what" and "why" of the activities, embedded in a five-phase process model (see Sect. 3).

To verify and validate its design, we separately developed three implementation strategies (see Sect. 4), for three different non-public higher education institutions, namely the "Copernicus" Wroclaw Computer Science and Management University (WSZI), WSB University in Gdansk (WSB) and Jan Wyżykowski University (UJW). By adopting a qualitative study design, as an exploratory, descriptive approach, in the first step we collected all of the necessary data, using a specific thematic approach, while in the second step we analyzed the data in a fashion reflecting the aim of recognizing circumstances and challenges related to the subject matter.

It is worth noting here that nowadays, non-public universities play an essential role in higher education [41–43] and have to compete very hard in order to gather potential students [44–46]. Their position increasingly depends on the quality of the education and the managerial competencies of the university governance [47–49]. In both cases, applying intelligent technologies seems to be a must if one considers their competitiveness and development. Yet, the level of its implementation is still relatively low in comparison with the business sector.

On the other hand, there are a few cases documented, giving an idea in which areas AI methods have been implemented within higher education institutions (HEIs) [50–52]. In particular, intelligent technologies are gradually being implemented in non-public universities [53], usually being part of the strategy that sets up a framework of priorities [54]. However, to the best of our knowledge, very few studies have considered the benefits and challenges affecting the implementation of AI technologies within university emerging set-ups.

The rest of the paper is structured as follows. Section 2 discusses artificial intelligence (AI) in the education sector, introducing the basic concepts, benefits and challenges related to its implementation, as well as a discussion of modern AI systems and tools. Section 3 presents a strategy implementation model, conceptualized by a five-stage generic process along with the corresponding configuration guide. Section 4 describes and analyzes the case studies, illustrating how AI implementations, based on underlying decision processes, are conducted in practice. Finally, we conclude in Sect. 5.

2   AI in Education

By design, intelligent technology is a method which uses knowledge to achieve concrete purpose in efficiency. At present, there are the following intelligent technologies: multi-agent, machine learning, ontology, semantic and knowledge grid, autonomic computing, cognitive informatics and neural computing. The prompt advances in these fields have already brought substantial changes in education, opening up new opportunities and challenges to teach and learn anytime and anywhere by providing new methods and systems that aim to stimulate innovative teaching and ultimately improve learning outcomes.

2.1   AI Concepts

The continuous progress of modern information technologies is strictly connected with the presence of implemented artificial intelligence techniques. During the over 60 years of development of artificial intelligence, several intelligent approaches have appeared in almost all sectors of modern life. Therefore, one can talk about the new generation of AI, including the potential power of the current solutions and the variety of applied techniques. The crucial components of such an understanding of AI 3.0 are presented in Fig. 1.

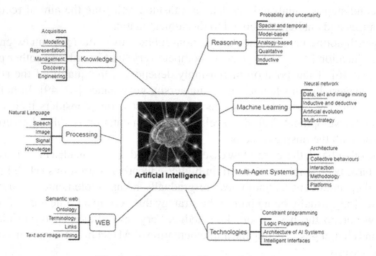

Fig. 1. Artificial intelligence 3.0 [55].

Particular categories of AI can be combined in the final applications; some of them seem to be obligatory (knowledge, reasoning, processing) while others are employed for the specific solutions where knowledge should be permanently updated (machine learning) or requires cooperation between specialized agents (multi-agent systems). Either way, the current solutions are not quite satisfactory – the level of the obtained progress is less than human intelligence. The next imaginable stages are still before us – we are heading toward Artificial Super Intelligence passing in the meantime through Artificial General Intelligence (see Fig. 2).

To sum up, the landscape of Artificial Intelligence in terms of using the main categories is rather stable. Yet, learning-based techniques are playing an increasingly significant role. However, the specialty of the application areas can determine the shape of implementation of artificial intelligence methods. The educational sector and the specifics of non-public universities are real determinants in defining the implementation of intelligent technologies.

2.2 AI Technologies

With the advent of AI in the mid-1950s to the present day, the proliferation of its methods and techniques has made it possible to develop intelligent systems which are increasingly relevant in education and training. For instance, Nuance, the high-tech company from Burlington (Massachusetts) [57], has implemented speech recognition software that can be used both by students and faculty. The application can transcribe up to 160 words per minute and is particularly useful for students who have limited mobility or struggle with

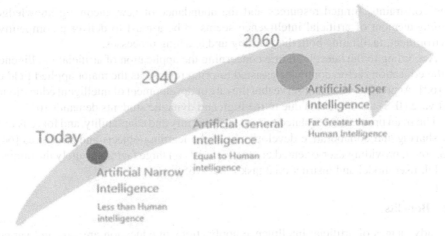

Fig. 2. Future evolution of artificial intelligence [56].

writing. The available features also enhance word recognition and spelling. Teachers can apply the software to prepare homework and assemble and schedule recurrent tasks such as sending notifications or emails.

Another company, Knewton, is promoting its newest product, Alta [58], as a complete courseware solution that combines expertly designed adaptive learning technology with high quality openly available content. In other words, Alta helps identify drawbacks in a student's knowledge by providing relevant coursework, and supports teaching activities at different educational levels.

Cognii is another provider of artificial intelligence by virtue of virtual assistants (VAs) that combine the powers of conversational pedagogy with the conversational AI technology [59]. Interestingly, the open-format applied to the VAs' responses is claimed to improve critical-thinking skills. The VAs also provide real-time feedback, and individual tutoring, customized to the particular student's requirements.

Querium, a successful start-up from Austin (Texas) [60], helps students master critical STEM skills by delivering a customizable STEM tutoring program of personalized and effective lessons which works on desktop computers and smart-phones. Querium's AI provides teachers with insights into the student's learning habits and highlights areas in which the student should improve.

Century is another successful start-up, established in 2013 in London by Priya Lakhani [61]. Behind its success is a diverse team of teachers, technologists, neuroscientists and parents. Their platform utilizes data analytics and cognitive neuroscience to create personalized learning plans and reduce workloads for teachers. Moreover, the AI platform tracks student progress, identifies knowledge gaps and delivers personal learning recommendations and feedback. The teacher dashboard allows them to monitor individual student and whole-class performance.

These examples show only some of the possible applications of AI in the education sector. Nevertheless, we argue that the above allows us to claim that at a general level, the constellation of AI methods and tools leverage both learning and teaching. With time constraints, limited resources and the abundance of new, incoming knowledge, the engagement of artificial intelligence seems to be a must to deliver a competitive environment, facilitating both the learning and teaching processes.

According to the latest literature concerning the application of artificial intelligence in the education sector, computer-assisted tutoring represents the major applied field of AI [62]. At present, we can observe that the rate of development of intelligent educational software (IES) has increased due to the high and dynamic students demands [63].

The main problems are related to content flexibility and adaptability, and for reusability, sharing and collaborative development of the learning objects and structures [64]. Moreover, providing user-oriented content depends on three factors, namely the domain model, user model and instructional task model [65].

2.3 Benefits

The advantages of artificial intelligence applications in education are vast and varied. Here, everything can be considered to be beneficial if we are thinking of anything, for example a computer program, that can efficiently perform any task that would normally rely on the intelligence of a human. Based on the state-of-the art research in this area, we outline nine areas in which AI methods can bring added value for both learning and teaching activities [66].

The first benefit concerns automated grading which simulates the behavior of a teacher to assign grades to the answer sheets submitted by the students. It can assess their knowledge by processing and analyzing their answers, giving feedback and recommending personalized teaching plans.

Secondly, intermediate spaced repetition aims at knowledge revision when someone is just about to forget. It is worth noting that Polish inventor Peter Wozniak [67] introduced the SuperMemo application, which is based on the effect of spaced repetition. The app keeps track of what a user is learning, and when he/she is doing it. By applying AI techniques, the application can discover when a user is most likely about to forget something and recommend revising it.

Thirdly, feedback loops for teachers, aided by machine learning and natural language processing techniques, improves the quality of student evaluations. For example, a chatbot can collect opinions via a dialog interface similarly to a real interviewer but with a small amount of work required by the user. Moreover, each conversation can be adapted according to the student's personality and provided answers. A chatbot can even formulate the reasons for particular opinions.

Fourthly, to support teachers in their classroom work, one can put into use virtual facilitators. For instance, at the Georgia Institute of Technology on Knowledge-Based Artificial Intelligence (KBAI) class, students were introduced to a new teacher's assistant named Jill Watson (JW) [68], who has been operating on the online discussion forums of different offerings of the KBAI class since Spring 2016. JW autonomously responded to student introductions, answered routine, frequently asked questions, and posted announcements on a weekly basis.

In the fifth place, Watts introduced chat campus based on the IBM Watson cognitive computing technologies [69]. In brief, students at Deakin University have asked IBM Watson 1600 questions a week to learn the ins and outs of life on campus and studying in the cloud. Within 12 months of implementing Watson, due to the enhanced quality of the student know-how at Deakin, this ground-breaking solution has handled more than 55,000 questions from students. Furthermore, the school is progressing its use of Watson, broadening its capabilities and teaching the system to understand new sources of information.

Personalized learning is the sixth example of AI applications in the education sector. In general, it refers to a variety of educational programs in which the pace of learning and the instructional approach are customized and eventually optimized for the needs of each learner [70]. In particular, the content is tailored to the learning preferences and specific interests of each student.

The seventh example—one of the most promising—is adaptive learning (AL). While the traditional model of classroom education, continues to be very much one-size-fits-all, on the contrary, AI-powered AL systems are designed to optimize learning efficiency. For example, Yixue Squirrel AI (Yixue) collects and analyses students' behavior data, updates learner profiles, then accordingly provides timely individualized feedback to each student [71].

Since cheating is a concern for all teachers, AI-powered anti-cheating systems have been presented as another (eighth) application of AI in the education sector. Proctoring is software which secures the authenticity of the test taker and prevent him/her from cheating as a proctor is always present during the test [72].

The last solution argued by Watts is data accumulation and personalization. For instance, learning grammatical rules can be aided by examples only from the domain being the subject of personal interest [73].

2.4 Challenges

There are several approaches to planning and organizing the implementation of AI methods in the education domain [6, 31, 50, 74–78], but discussion about the essential challenges for decision-makers is still ongoing. To the best of our knowledge, the list of potential challenges that influence the implementation of intelligent technologies concern:

- **strategy** refers to a general plan of implementation to achieve one or more specific long-term goals accordingly to a schedule established and agreed with all interested stakeholders;
- **organizational maturity** refers to its employees, processes and technology readiness and capability with respect to the adoption of artificial intelligence technologies;
- **data governance**, refers to data principles, quality, meta-data, access requirements and data life cycle; since machines learn on the basis of data, data governance is a crucial facet of the implementation and further maintenance of AI;
- **infrastructure**, being the combination of hardware and software systems, is particularly acute due to compatibility and integration issues.

As one would expect, it is important to establish a strategy that defines the goals with regard to the AI implementation and provides a means to manage them. The strategy itself might take the form of a mix of qualitative and quantitative approaches. The former aims to describe how the goals will be fulfilled, while the latter aims to decide if the goals are fulfilled and which goals are fulfilled. The fulfilment of the goals cab be expressed in quantitative numbers, or/and in qualitative terms.

In general, maturity is a synonym of "full development" or "perfected condition," and since any organization is a living entity, it grows over a period of time and learn from its decisions and outcomes. Therefore, all organizations seem to be at some stage of maturity, striving forward to development and perfection. From a strategic point of view, we stress the importance of the high level of organizational maturity due to the changes spanning across core dimensions of strategic management such as: alignment, performance measurement and management, process improvement and sustainability. In the context of our study, maturity assessment should encompass external and internal benchmarks, describing the organization readiness and capability to adopt AI technologies.

Another challenge is data governance, which is related to the system of data organization, collection, control, storage, usage, archival and destruction. The path of setting up data governance is driven by a specific program, supported by particular policies and procedures, and communicated by organizational leadership and management. In general, the regulations must provide all of the necessary means to preserve the following generic requirements: accessibility, availability, completeness, accuracy, integrity, consistency, auditability, and security.

The last, but not least significant, challenge concerns the infrastructure which encompasses all of the hardware installations and the software entities. Recent advancements in the artificial intelligence technology landscape have introduced specific requirements toward hardware capacity and software capabilities. In an effort to integrate these cutting-edge technologies with the existing systems, one has to incorporate solutions that underpin a flexible and scalable end-to-end integration. Enabling on-the-fly software asset configurations and reconfigurations (in the case of enabling/disabling particular services) facilitates an "assembly-from-parts" model for implementing new and updating existing AI applications from a catalog of services.

We argue that the above-mentioned challenges are essential to take into consideration while preparing the discussed scenarios (see Sect. 4). Our research in essence attempts to identify and analyze the issues related to implementing AI in education, however it still lacks the empirical evidence which might at least confirm our perceptions of the studied phenomenon.

3 Strategy Implementation Model

Undoubtedly, artificial intelligence has had significant influence on various industries, leveraging their effectiveness, productivity and profitability. This also applies to the education sector which has been committed to several reforms, addressing key sectoral issues and including incorporating artificial intelligence tools and methods.

It is believed that such a shift will bring a new perspective to many facets of existing learning and teaching techniques. Toumi, in his report from 2018, claims that [67]: "(...) in the domain of educational policy, it is important for educators and policymakers to understand AI in the broader context of the future of learning. (...) As AI will be used to automate productive processes, we may need to reinvent current educational institutions. (...)."

This opinion and many others thereafter argue the need to better comprehend the impact of artificial intelligence on education. However, first we need to develop a model that will drive the process of implementation and result in the smooth deployment of AI systems. At this point, we argue that the below model is suitable under general contexts, and is thus applicable to any organization.

The five-stage process shown in Fig. 3 organizes, arranges and systematizes the tasks into consequent groups. The particular tasks employed in each stage might cross other phases, to an extent which depends on the context of the implementation (e.g. strategy, organizational maturity, data governance). Therefore, the five stages are interdependent with each other, whereas the duration and labor intensity may significantly vary. The model of the implementation process consists of five stages:

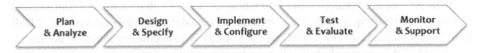

Fig. 3. General strategy implementation model.

1. **Plan and analyze** stage concerns all activities associated with the creation and maintenance of a plan which describes a list of steps with details of the timing and resources required to achieve the desired goals, along with the budget and general time frames.
2. **Design and specify** stage aims to prepare and establish the structure and organization of the system as well as to define the functional and non-functional requirements. In other words, a specification should address all enumerated goals in the first stage.
3. **Implement and configure** stage can be interpreted twofold; the system implementation is the process of creating its source code by the software developers, or the system implementation is installing and configuring the software applications.
4. **Test and evaluate** stage aims to ensure that the actual software is free of defects, and to check and determine whether it matches the expected requirements, as defined in the second phase.
5. **Monitor and support** stage concerns the surveillance process on measurable events regarding the performance of the system, as well as providing assistance and help to the users of the system required due to any issues and incidents encountered.

Moreover, it should be emphasized that it is necessary to identify the specificities of AI software and evaluate existing resources, including hardware capacity, software compatibility and IT personnel. However, anticipating all of the relevant resources is only possible under exceptional circumstances exceptionally possible due to uncertainty regarding especially the human factor and data quality (used to teach AI algorithms).

3.1 Implementation Strategy Configuration

One should keep in mind that the strategy is a "how" the goals (objectives) will be achieved by the means (resources). In the context of this study, the strategy consists of the desired objectives and corresponding actions in order to implement an AI solution. Having said that, the structure of the implementation configuration is as follows:

- general purpose and vision,
- scope, specific objectives with priorities and within time frames,
- reference to the procedures used, regarding all five stages of the implementation model (see Fig. 3),
- reference to the AI systems, services and tools which are existing and able to be included in the strategic plan, or in the case of developing a new system, a description of the possible software vendors, trusted advisors and consultancy agencies, and individuals experts, all with designated roles and responsibilities.

This perspective conceives the know-how as a highly deliberate, descriptive, and logical one, involving a sequential, rational and analytical collaborative work of all interested stakeholders. The configuration strategy is conceptually aimed at achieving the master plan by precisely following the implementation process.

However, this form of strategy configuration can be mostly applied in organizations which at least manage projects in accordance with a policy that aims to identify and monitor the progress towards project performance objectives (level two).

4   Exploratory Multiple Case Study

Respecting the autonomy of higher education institutions, we would expect very individual approaches to deploying a single or suite of AI techniques for the university. The selected non-public universities that participated in the research are different in terms of geneses, formal statements as well as levels of computer infrastructure and areas of education. Before presenting the proposals for implementing artificial intelligence solutions in the inquired HEIs, short descriptions of the universities are delivered, focusing on their areas and levels of education. The state-of-the-art regarding the maturity of the implemented IT solutions are also discussed.

4.1   Case Settings

Case 1. WSZI in Wroclaw. The university which is the subject of research of this article, namely The "Copernicus" University of Information Technology and Management, has been operating on the educational services market for nearly 20 years and is one of 384 non-public universities in Poland.

Since 2001, it has educated 4,000 graduates, mainly in the area of new technologies. Further observations and conclusions presented in the article will be based only on their own observations of business practice and the environment and competition due to the lack of data from external actors evaluating the quality, innovation and conditions for studying and living for students. Starting from 2019, the university has been conducting studies solely in the field of Computer Science in a full-time and part-time system at two levels, including post-graduate studies and courses.

The organizational structure of the university is a simplified structure with one department and full decision-making ability of the Chancellor, who is also the founder. His decisions are binding on financial, program and student matters. For the analysis of the organizational structure, one can state that WSIZ "Copernicus" omits the very important role of Rector. Usually, the rector in a non-public university is the person who deals with the organization of education and training, but his decisions are not binding without the authorization of the Chancellor. In addition, the described university is a unit educating a total of about 700 students in a full-time and part-time systems.

Among others: the department of the Rector's office, where there are too few employees and students. It is worth noting that if there were changes in the functioning of the organizational structure, it could be possible to reorganize the work and introduce intelligent technologies into these structures, introducing the innovation which would lead to the beginning of changes.

The financing of a non-public university, which clearly affects the development and functioning of educational institutions, departs from the possibility of financing public entities. Obtaining funds or research grants is difficult due to the small number of students.

There is also no obligation to conduct research, which makes it more difficult to win in competitions. All retrofitting of the university halls are covered only from the profit earned, which consists of tuition payment and fees for program differences, conditions. When it comes to the issue of payment for tuition, the student has the privilege of financing science on the basis of a scholarships obtained, which are largely similar in terms of the procedures for obtaining funds in public universities.

A non-public university, even though it is a university, is also an enterprise. And just as a company will not exist without clients, a private university will not be able to break out of the educational market without the influence and opinion of its potential future students.

If we focus our conclusions on the differences in the functioning of these two types of universities, we should also mention the change in the law on higher education, which imposed student limits per lecturer on public universities. In WSIZ "Copernicus", the current number of students per lecturer is 25–30 students, which definitely departs from the provisions of law for public entities.

In addition, due to the lack of sufficiently qualified teaching staff and the Chancellor's desire to reduce employee costs, the university introduced the possibility of writing diploma theses to teachers with a master's degree, provided that formal care over diploma theses will be carried out by a promoter with a doctorate degree. However, he leads the student through the whole process of writing the work, advises him, gives his opinion on his progress and is listed in the diploma documentation. The content supervisor, who is subject to the promoter, is a person with a doctorate degree or above. Such a solution is allowed by the applicable law and applied in WSIZ "Copernicus", however, there is no information whether and to what extent public HEIs use it.

Looking at the above information about the structure, method of financing and processes taking place in the area of education and work organization of the described non-public university, it can be stated that although it is an entity educating students similarly to state universities, it is significantly different from them.

Obviously, it is not disputed that issues such as legal regulations, the shape and form of the graduate and student documents, requirements regarding ECTS points, and reporting or deadlines, are almost identical. However, they are so individual in their approach to the quality of education and the candidate that each of them should be considered separately. In the same way, when designing and implementing business analytics solutions, it should be taken into account that what works in a given non-public unit does not necessarily have to serve another organization, especially a state one.

Case 2. WSB University in Gdansk. The WSB Universities is the largest group of university schools of business in Poland. All of them are found in top positions in rankings of higher education institutions. Founded in 1994 by TEB Akademia, WSB launched its first field of study: "finance and banking". Presently, the WSB Universities are located in 10 cities across Poland: Gdańsk and Gdynia, Bydgoszcz and Toruń, Wrocław, Chorzów, Opole, Poznań, Szczecin, and Warszawa.

The organization of this particular University is typical for HEIs in Poland. The faculties and departments are oriented on educational sectors and there are many supporting divisions mentioned in the characteristics of the previous University, but particular units cooperate strongly, including by utilizing common platforms (webpages) for students and academic staff.

The WSB educational offer covers both bachelor's and master's programs. The duration of the former is 3 years (6 semesters) while the latter is 2 years long. It is worth noting here that a student can pursue second-cycle programs in a field that is not directly related to that of their first-cycle degree. In that way, one can extend their area of professional expertise and hence enhance their employability. Each program is focused on developing practical competencies and soft skills.

Each university is governed by their own statutes and regulations, but are integral to the make-up of the ownership authorities. Moreover, each individual university has its own internal procedures, regulations, and local authorities. The university is governed by the rector along with the chancellor. At the head of each faculty are the dean and vice-deans, supported by the proxies.

University Faculties organize teaching and research into individual domains, or groups of subjects. Their work is normally organized into subdivisions called departments. The University's administrative and support departments support the running of the University and contribute to research, teaching and international cooperation with other universities worldwide.

The organization claims to maintain a high performance culture that is inspirational and motivating, providing internal and external funds to support faculty staff development. The aim of each subsidiary is to provide an attractive, sustainable, vibrant, and accessible campus, upheld by a contemporary virtual environment in which students, staff, and engaged stakeholders can interact, and share information and knowledge.

Case 3. Jan Wyżykowski University in Polkowice. Jan Wyżykowski University was created thanks to the cooperation of Polkowice Commune and Polkowice County. The founder of the University is the ZAMPOL company, which Polkowice Commune and Polkowice County own all of the shares of. Currently, UJW runs studies within the

Bachelor's, Engineer's, Master's programmes and postgraduate studies and courses of Education offerings: Bachelor's studies (3-year studies) in the fields of: Administration, Pedagogy and Management. Engineer's studies (3.5-year studies) in the fields of: Information Technology, Mechatronics, Logistics, Mining and Geology, Production Management and Engineering. Master's studies in the fields of Management (2-year), Mechatronics (1.5-year) and a uniform (5-year studies Law) are the newest in the offer.

All educational majors are offered as extramural studies, so basically, students gain practical experience working for different companies. The second important feature of the university is that it acts in a very specific region known from its copper industry. Most of the students are employed in companies connected with this industry so their professional expectations are strictly tied with copper infrastructure or reflect more general positions typical for medium-sized cities (administration and management).

Nowadays, the information systems present in UJW support typical transaction processes: student enrollment, planning and evidence of classes and some functions offering by online education. It is quite a well-functioning university information systems but without functionality specific for AI methods.

4.2 Implementation Strategies Settings

The solutions in Fig. 4 use the latest technologies, which confirms that many repetitive tasks and procedures could benefit from the support of AI systems, thus offering new development opportunities and fields of study for higher education.

It is important to remember that there are many often more complex and non-standard procedures at universities. The processes of obtaining the intended effects from the implementation of the proposed solutions based on AI should be in accordance with applicable standards and the law regarding higher education and also take into account the capabilities of the university. Each replacement or support through the implementation of technological innovations is intended to shorten the time of document circulation, reduce administrative costs and improve the quality of education, which is certainly worthy of attention.

Naturally, introducing such a solution based on new technology solutions is not without its own inherent risks. Non-public universities would need to exercise extreme caution in protecting students' personal data and would need some level of human oversight to monitor every AI method.

Case 1. WSIZ University. Building creative solutions into the work of a non-public university is also helpful in creating new products and services. The implementation of smart technology solutions at a private university will foster the building of scientific and educational progress, which will translate into satisfactory financial results and will strengthen the position on the non-public university market and introduce the element of innovation to the current activities of the unit. As part of the implementation work envisaged at the "Copernicus" University of Information Technology and Management in Wroclaw, it is planned to create a chatbot—an intelligent application for managing responses and relations with students and candidates for studies.

THE NEED TO
IMPLEMENT AI
SOLUTION

pre-implementation
analysis

CONCEPT

- preparation of the AI solution concept ba sed on:
- number of students
- size of a private tmiversity
- number of employees
- implementation costs
- integ:.-ation with current software

WSIZ	WSB	UJW
AI solution: Automation of signing contrncb• for 1e::tnling in educational units	AI solution: Automatic checking of otntlent attendance	AI solution: Automated p↑epu-::ltion for the!>:i defense —*DJplomant UJW*
Automation of the signing contract would take place in the following steps: **-to the e-mail address provided in the recruitment form there is a link to the page with a learning contract asking for familiarization with its content,** **-after learning the terms of the contract, the student is asked to accept it through the "I accept the terms of the learning contract• button,** **- if you select this be an agreement concluded in electronic form to legal consequences resulting from its signing.**	**The application allows** you to **automatically check the presence of** students during lectures by logging **students into the wtive:rsity network.** Data on the people present during classes are traosferred directly to the **university management system and made available to lecrurers**	Each of the graduates after submitting their work at the deao's office, by logging **in** to the *Dyplomant UJW* app will be able to check progress in preparation **for the defense of the thesis.** The application **will automatically notifY the student about** sending the \Vork for review and about **thegrade. In the next stepthe app will send a message about the date of thesis defense and about the dare of receipt of the diploma**

Discussing the implern.enbtion phn

Installation of the AI solution

Configuration and integration with the current university system

Testiug and correction of reported errors of AI solution

Implementation

Testiug and correction of reported errors of AI solution

VERIFICATION OF IMPLEMENTATION
- ftmctional check of AI solution
- maintaining the state after implementation

Fig. 4. Scenarios of implementation of selected AI methods for WSIZ, WSB and UJW.

This solution, in connection with the personnel problems of the non-public university described would answer simple questions about the dates of the sessions, exams, classes and inform about the recruitment schedule and the recruitment documents needed. As part of the planned implementation, it is also planned to reorganize the signing of learning contracts, which would consist in enabling their signing in electronic form via a link sent, generated by the internal university system, which is consistent with the provision in art. 60 cc. Support for such a contract would take place in the following steps:

1. A link would be sent to the student's e-mail address to the page about the learning contract with a request to read its contents.
2. After learning the terms of the contract, the student would be asked to accept it by clicking the "I accept the terms of the learning contract" button.
3. After choosing this option, the contract is concluded electronically. Afterwards, the student accepts the presented conditions, the confirmation along with the contract is sent automatically in a pdf file to the dean's employee. It is then printed and archived to the student's personal file.

In addition, the plans of AI implementation in WSIZ also include the preparation and full implementation of a voice guide for students and candidates with impaired vision. The voice guide presents an educational offer and discusses payment, calls the phone number for the department, and checks the plan for that academic year.

The introduction of intelligent solutions for the work of the "Copernicus" University of Information Technology and Management in Wroclaw creates opportunities to facilitate procedures in the recruitment process, and reduce the use of office machines, which also affects the improvement of the environment. It relieves the work of the dean's office, which is the most important area in contact with students and candidates.

Of course, apart from the positive aspects, one may ask the question whether intelligent technologies strive to improve human work and make it easier for them to complete certain processes to become more attractive on the market, or whether it is simply interference in human work and increasing unemployment. However, believing only in the good aspects of the case, we believe that the solutions and techniques of business intelligence will significantly improve the quality of the education process and assist in acquiring new students at the "Copernicus" University of Information Technology and Management in Wroclaw.

Case 2. WSB Universities. We have identified three administrative areas which are planned to be fully or partially automated by implementing artificial intelligence tools. The list is given below (not in order of priority).

1. **Grouping, sorting and responding to emails.** From our employees, we know that replying to emails is a time-consuming job. Moreover, repetitive email conversations are also frustrating and can be demotivating in the longterm. There are a number of tools which are being considered to be included in a pilot study, namely: AI Email Smart Answer [79], OMQ Reply [80], and Notion [81]. All of these tools are able to automate responses to emails and eventually replace the manual work of employees. Recurrent students' requests are automatically recognized and answered

by the system. Obviously, the list of features of the AI-powered solutions doesn't end here.

2. **Scheduling appointments.** Scheduling meetings with multiple students is a labor-intensive task. We believe that instead of manually responding via email to schedule an appointment and check the calendars of everyone involved, we could implement intelligent agents that detect and recognize certain phases in incoming emails, eventually proposing appointment times according to individual availability, and schedule appointments based on the attendees' responses. Again, we have selected a few tools which are planned to be tested in a pilot study, namely: Julie Desk [82], ArtiBot [83], and Hendrix.ai [84]. Meetings are still a crucial method of organizing and planning work, but they are a waste of time unless one accurately captures what was discussed and agreed upon. By design, the agents require access to individual calendars, email accounts, social media profiles and location data to provide the necessary data to the AI-based inference engine. In return, they simply serve as virtual assistants, capable of preparing meetings, dialing into conference calls, turning on a video projectors, loading presentations, removing outdated and duplicate contacts, and many more otherwise tedious tasks.

3. **Customer service AI chatbot.** A chatbot is simply a software agent that can simulate a conversation with a user in natural language in a real time trough messaging applications, websites, mobile applications, or even over the telephone. The requests reported by the students dramatically increase before particular events, such as bachelor and master diploma exams, the beginning and the end of the academic year, as well as from the candidates who intend to become students. Therefore, customer service employees are regularly inundated with follow-up calls, support requests, frequently and repetitively asked questions, confirmation emails, complaints, and many more. To face these issues, IBM tells us that "chatbots can help businesses save on customer service costs by speeding up response times, freeing up agents for more challenging work, and answering up to 80% of routine questions" [85].

Moreover, unlike live agents (employees), software agents don't need lunch hours or coffee breaks, and are not absent due to holidays, or illness, or any other natural disasters which can put human lives at risk. At the moment, our pilot study includes the following AI chatbot software to be tested: ActiveChat [86], Respond.io [31], and ChatBot [88]. We expect to uncover sizeable advantages by implementing chatbots across the organization.

On the other hand, we are aware that it will not be an easy and effortless task. On the contrary, based on our learnings, we have identified and listed the following three major challenges, namely: security and privacy, obstacles and burdens due to polish language complexity, data input for machine learning algorithms. Undoubtedly, chatbots are one of the most promising enterprise AI technologies, however, achieving maximum business value from them requires from us extensive work and persevering determination.

Case 3. UJW University. Nowadays, the UJW educational unit is trying to be competitive as a local experimental HEI. Therefore, the educational offering relates to regional needs especially strongly connected with the copper industry and other companies located in the region. UJW was a leader of Erasmus grants devoted to improving the educational level through applying new teaching methods using AI (e.g. project DIMBI

[89] and related [90–93]). Therefore all potential solutions in this HEI are strictly connected with the results of these projects extended by discovered niches in education. Three directions of AI techniques to embrace are:

1. **Using innovative methods of teaching selected courses.** At the beginning, practical abilities and skills refer to the data science and mechatronic majors.
2. **Smart agents** (SAs). SAs are used to automate administrative procedures with the aim to simplify daily tasks.
3. **Chatbots.** Implementation of chatbots for communication with actual and potential students. This project is comparable to that presented in the previous universities.

Educating staff for the constantly changing trends and creating innovations both in the area of education and the functioning of a private educational unit translates into profit and brand visibility and the prestige of education. The search for creative solutions is the equation between the known, acceptable order and the chaos that innovation can bring. However, if innovation is treated as a course of action, as a way of managing, without worrying about disturbing relative stability, after a period of time, it can be seen that it has marked out new directions and possibilities of creating a competitive advantage.

To sum up, we think that the automation of a universities' administrative tasks and customization of their student-oriented activities are not only possible, but imminent. The goal of AI technologies is to make human-like judgments and perform tasks in order to downsize employees' workloads. Today, academic communities are intensively developing and studying this field of AI applications. Indeed, the findings from research commissioned by the Microsoft show almost complete acceptance among educators that AI is important for their future—"99.4 percent said AI would be instrumental to their institution's competitiveness within the next three years, with 15 per cent calling it a game-changer" [94].

However, in this paper, including the assumptions of the first pilot study, we "only" considered selected administrative areas, performed by the employees not directly responsible for education. Nevertheless, we believe that AI has far-reaching potential to change the way of teaching and learning. Undeniably, the incoming shift has its advocates and opponents whose proofs and claims should be always carefully judged.

5   Conclusions

As the technologies of artificial intelligence evolved, so did the domains and practices of their implementation in education. Current trends have imposed new requirements on the organization and management of both teaching and learning. There are three interrelated aspects of this, one of which arises from the recent advancements and innovations of the cutting-edge machine learning methods and Internet-of-Things devices.

Secondly, the focus of both teachers and learners concern very large volumes of information and knowledge resources, freely available on the Web. Their growth in size and number seems to be an endless road to discover, but there is more and more evidence to help us pick the right direction. Thirdly, currently the competitiveness of higher educational institutions depends strongly on the increase in the effectiveness of learning methods, strongly supported by AI technologies and tools [95–97].

At a time when many education entities are stretched to capacity, and learners experience long wait times for on-site counseling, AI solutions could provide some facilities. It is therefore recommended that organizations should use solutions that are supported by the latest technological solutions, in order to improve the quality of education, and to minimize errors in the circulation of administrative documentation and the course of study.

To sum up, we argue that the role and impact of artificial intelligence has increased in the education and learning contexts. The academic sphere is becoming more effective and personalized on the one hand, as well as global, context-intensive (multi-cultural) and asynchronous on the other. The intersection of three areas, namely data, computation and education has set far-reaching consequences, raising fundamental question about the nature of teaching: what is taught, when it is taught, and how it is taught.

References

1. Bullock, L.: The top 6 ways that artificial intelligence will affect your business in the near future. Forbes Mag. https://www.forbes.com/sites/lilachbullock/2019/02/25/the-top-6-ways-that-artificial-intelligence-will-affect-your-business-in-the-near-future/
2. Hao, K.: China has started a grand experiment in AI education: it could reshape how the world learns. MIT Technol. Rev. 1 (2019)
3. Garrett, N., Beard, N., Fiesler, C.: More than "if time allows" the role of ethics in AI education. In: Proceedings of the AAAI/ACM Conference on AI, Ethics, and Society, pp. 272–278 (2020)
4. Neller, T.W.: AI education: birds of a feather. AI Matters 2(4), 7–8 (2016)
5. Forbes: Artificial Intelligence in Education Transformation (2020). https://www.forbes.com/sites/forbestechcouncil/2020/06/08/artificial-intelligence-in-education-transformation/#43ee5fb832a4
6. Yoon, D.M., Kim, K.J.: Challenges and opportunities in game artificial intelligence education using Angry Birds. IEEE Access 3, 793–804 (2015)
7. Kim, M.J., Kim, K.J., Kim, S., Dey, A.K.: Performance evaluation gaps in a real-time strategy game between human and artificial intelligence players. IEEE Access 6, 13575–13586 (2018)
8. Hernes, M.: A cognitive integrated management support system for enterprises. In: Hwang, D., Jung, J.J., Nguyen, N.-T. (eds.) ICCCI 2014. LNCS (LNAI), vol. 8733, pp. 252–261. Springer, Cham (2014). https://doi.org/10.1007/978-3-319-11289-3_26
9. Hernes, M., Sobieska-Karpińska, J.: Application of the consensus method in a multiagent financial decision support system. IseB 14(1), 167–185 (2015). https://doi.org/10.1007/s10257-015-0280-9
10. Nieto, Y., Gacía-Díaz, V., Montenegro, C., González, C.C., Crespo, R.G.: Usage of machine learning for strategic decision making at higher educational institutions. IEEE Access 7, 75007–75017 (2019)
11. Stimpson, A.J., Cummings, M.L.: Assessing intervention timing in computer-based education using machine learning algorithms. IEEE Access 2, 78–87 (2014)
12. Forbus, K.D., Feltovich, P.J.: Smart Machines in Education: The Coming Revolution in Educational Technology. MIT Press, Cambridge (2001)
13. Spasic, V.A.: Intelligent virtual systems in learning [and biomedical application]. In: Proceedings of the 22nd Annual International Conference of the IEEE Engineering in Medicine and Biology Society (Cat. No. 00CH37143), vol. 2, pp. 1016–1018. IEEE (2000)

14. McArthur, D., Lewis, M., Bishary, M.: The roles of artificial intelligence in education: current progress and future prospects. J. Educ. Technol. **1**(4), 42–80 (2005)
15. Payr, S.: The virtual university's faculty: an overview of educational agents. Appl. Artif. Intell. **17**(1), 1–19 (2003)
16. Kim, Y., Soyata, T., Behnagh, R.F.: Towards emotionally aware AI smart classroom: current issues and directions for engineering and education. IEEE Access **6**, 5308–5331 (2018)
17. Li, Y., Sun, Z., Han, L., Mei, N.: Fuzzy comprehensive evaluation method for energy management systems based on an Internet of Things. IEEE Access **5**, 21312–21322 (2017)
18. Gawin, B., Marcinkowski, B.:Towards a proficient business intelligence for energy efficiency domain–prerequisites and data sources. In: ICTM 2016, p. 73 (2016)
19. Marcinkowski, B., Gawin, B.: Business intelligence competency center–establishing the assets behind delivering analytic business value. In: ICT Management for Global Competitiveness and Economic Growth in Emerging Economies (ICTM), p. 224 (2017)
20. Owoc, M.L.: Intelligent paradigm in grid computing. Prace Naukowe Uniwersytetu Ekonomicznego we Wrocławiu. Knowl. Acquisition Manag. (25), 113–121 (2008)
21. Li, X., Huang, Q., Wu, D.: Distributed large-scale co-simulation for IoT-aided smart grid control. IEEE Access **5**, 19951–19960 (2017)
22. Marciniak, K., Owoc, M.L.: Usability of knowledge grid in smart city concepts. In: ICEIS, no. 3, pp. 341–346 (2013)
23. Owoc, M., Hauke, K., Weichbroth, P.: Knowledge-grid modelling for academic purposes. In: Mercier-Laurent, E., Boulanger, D. (eds.) AI4KM 2015. IAICT, vol. 497, pp. 1–14. Springer, Cham (2016). https://doi.org/10.1007/978-3-319-55970-4_1
24. Jakubczyc, J.A., Owoc, M.L.: Knowledge management and artificial intelligence. Argumenta Oeconomica **1**(6) (1998)
25. Jakubczyc, J.A., Matouk, K., Owoc, M.L.: Sukcesy i porażki systemów inteligentnych w Polsce: badania wstępne. Prace Naukowe Akademii Ekonomicznej we Wrocławiu. Nowoczesne technologie informacyjne w zarządzaniu (955), 331–344 (2002)
26. Owoc, M.L.: Wartościowanie wiedzy w inteligentnych systemach wspomagających zarządzanie. Prace Naukowe Akademii Ekonomicznej we Wrocławiu. Seria: Monografie i Opracowania (no 100), (1047) (2004)
27. Owoc, M., Marciniak, K.: Knowledge management as foundation of smart university. In: 2013 Federated Conference on Computer Science and Information Systems, pp. 1267–1272. IEEE (2013)
28. Sklar, E., Eguchi, A., Johnson, J.: RoboCupJunior: learning with educational robotics. In: Kaminka, G.A., Lima, P.U., Rojas, R. (eds.) RoboCup 2002. LNCS (LNAI), vol. 2752, pp. 238–253. Springer, Heidelberg (2003). https://doi.org/10.1007/978-3-540-45135-8_18
29. Blanchard, E.G., Volfson, B., Hong, Y.J., Lajoie, S.P.: Affective artificial intelligence in education: from detection to adaptation. In: AIEDm, vol. 2009, pp. 81–88 (2009)
30. McLaren, B.M., Scheuer, O., Mikšátko, J.: Supporting collaborative learning and e-discussions using artificial intelligence techniques. Int. J. Artif. Intell. Educ. **20**(1), 1–46 (2010)
31. Chen, L., Chen, P., Lin, Z.: Artificial intelligence in education: a review. IEEE Access **8**, 75264–75278 (2020)
32. Kapłański, P., Seganti, A., Cieśliński, K., Chrabrowa, A., Ługowska, I.: Automated reasoning based user interface. Expert Syst. Appl. **71**, 125–137 (2017)
33. Kaplanski, P., Weichbroth, P.: Cognitum ontorion: knowledge representation and reasoning system. In: Pełech-Pilichowski, T., Mach-Król, M., Olszak, C.M. (eds.) Advances in Business ICT: New Ideas from Ongoing Research. SCI, vol. 658, pp. 27–43. Springer, Cham (2017). https://doi.org/10.1007/978-3-319-47208-9_3
34. Weichbroth, P.: Fluent editor and controlled natural language in ontology development. Int. J. Artif. Intell. Tools **28**(04), 1940007 (2019)

35. Gołuchowski, J., Korzeb, M., Weichbroth, P.: Perspektywy wykorzystania architektury korporacyjnej w tworzeniu rozwiązań Smart City. Roczniki Kolegium Analiz Ekonomicznych. Szkoła Główna Handlowa (38), 86–98 (2015)
36. Duan, Y.Q., Fan, X.Y., Liu, J.C., Hou, Q.H.: Operating efficiency-based data mining on intensive land use in smart city. IEEE Access **8**, 17253–17262 (2020)
37. Kirimtat, A., Krejcar, O., Kertesz, A., Tasgetiren, M.F.: Future trends and current state of smart city concepts: a survey. IEEE Access **8**, 86448–86467 (2020)
38. Boiński, T.: Using open source components in software developement (2014)
39. Ossowska, K., Szewc, L., Weichbroth, P., Garnik, I., Sikorski, M.: Exploring an ontological approach for user requirements elicitation in the design of online virtual agents. In: Wrycza, S. (ed.) Information Systems: Development, Research, Applications, Education: 9th SIGSAND/PLAIS EuroSymposium 2016, Gdansk, Poland, September 29, 2016, Proceedings, pp. 40–55. Springer, Cham (2016). https://doi.org/10.1007/978-3-319-46642-2_3
40. Ai, J., Guo, H., Wong, W.E.: What ruined your cake: impacts of code modifications on bug distribution. IEEE Access **8**, 84020–84036 (2020)
41. Wells, P.J., Sadlak, J.: The rising role and relevance of private higher education in Europe. In: Vlasceanu, L. (ed.) UNESCO-CEPES, Bucharest (2007)
42. Slantcheva, S., Levy, D. (eds.): Private Higher Education in Post-Communist Europe: In Search of Legitimacy. Springer, New York (2007). https://doi.org/10.1057/9780230604391
43. Ajadi, T.O.: Private Universities in Nigeria–the Challenges Ahead. Am. J. Sci. Res. **1**(7), 1–10 (2010)
44. Jongbloed, B.: Regulation and competition in higher education. In: Teixeira, P., Jongbloed, B., Dill, D., Amaral, A. (eds.) Markets in Higer Education, pp. 87–111. Springer, Heidelberg (2004). https://doi.org/10.1007/1-4020-2835-0_5
45. Fazlagić, J., Skikiewicz, R.: The role of intellectual capital in building competitive advantage of non-public universities. In: Economic and Social Development: Book of Proceedings, p. 547 (2014)
46. Dakowska, D.: Competitive universities? The impact of international and European trends on academic institutions in the 'New Europe.' Euro. Educ. Res. J. **16**(5), 588–604 (2017)
47. Macukow, B.: Education quality assurance in the Warsaw University of Technology-prerequisites and activities already undertaken. Eur. J. Eng. Educ. **25**(1), 9–17 (2000)
48. Tabaku, E.: Service quality in higher education; analysis and comparison between public and non-public institutions. In: 5th International Conference on Contemporary Marketing Issues, ICCMI, Thessaloniki, Greece, 21–23 June 2017, p. 525 (2017)
49. Białoń, L.: Budowanie wizerunku szkoły wyższej jako mega narzędzia marketing. Marketing Instytucji Naukowo Badawczych. MINIB, Warszawa (2012)
50. Popenici, S.A.D, Kerr, S.: Exploring the impact of artificial intelligence on teaching and learning in higher education. Res. Pract. Technol. Enhanced Learn. **12**(1) (2017). Article number: 22. https://doi.org/10.1186/s41039-017-0062-8
51. Pedro, F., et al.: AI for Education: Challenges and Opportunities (2019). https://unesdoc.unesco.org/ark:/48223/pf0000366994
52. Sagenmuller, I.: How Artificial Intelligence helps Higher Education Management (2020). https://www.u-planner.com/en-us/blog/artificial-intelligence-use-in-higher-education-management
53. Accreditations, affiliations and quality. https://www.kozminski.edu.pl/en/about-kozminski/accreditations-affiliations-and-quality/crasp/
54. Wróblewska, W.: W poszukiwaniu uwarunkowań podwyższania jakości kształcenia w szkole wyższej. In: Grzesiak, J. (ed.) Ewaluacja poprawy jakości kształcenia, WPA UAM w Kaliszu & PWSZ w Koninie, Kalisz, Konin (2014)

55. Mercier-Laurent, E., Kayakutlu, G.: Proceedings of the 7th International Workshop on Artificial Intelligence for Knowledge Management (AI4KM 2017) AI for Humans, Melbourne, Australia (2017)
56. Ballant, C.: Artificial Intelligence, Machine Learning, and Deep Learning: Same Context, Different Concepts (2018). https://master-iesc-angers.com/artificial-intelligence-machine-learning-and-deep-learning-same-context-different-concepts/
57. Nuance (2020). https://www.nuance.com/about-us/who-we-are.html
58. Knewton (2020). https://www.knewton.com/
59. Cognii (2020). https://www.cognii.com/
60. Querium (2020). http://querium.com/
61. Century (2020). https://www.century.tech/
62. Unesco: Artificial intelligence in education: challenges and opportunities for sustainable development (2019). https://unesdoc.unesco.org/ark:/48223/pf0000366994
63. Kulkarni, A.: AI in Education: Where is It Now and What is the Future? (2019). https://www.lexalytics.com/lexablog/ai-in-education-present-future-ethics
64. Aroyo, L., Mizoguchi, R.: Authoring support framework for intelligent educational systems. In: Proccedings of AI in Education, AIED, pp. 362–364 (2003)
65. Thalheim, B.: The conceptual framework to user-oriented content management. In: Frontiers in Artificial Intelligence and Applications, vol. 154, p. 30 (2007)
66. Watts, E.: 9 ways to use Artificial Intelligence (AI) in education. https://bigdata-madesimple.com/9-ways-to-use-artificial-intelligence-in-education/
67. Wolf, G.: Want to Remember Everything You'll Ever Learn? Surrender to This Algorithm. https://www.wired.com/2008/04/ff-wozniak/
68. Goel, A.K., Polepeddi, L.: Jill Watson: a virtual teaching assistant for online education. Georgia Institute of Technology (2016)
69. IBM Watson helps Deakin drive the digital frontier. https://www.deakin.edu.au/about-deakin/media-releases/articles/ibm-watson-helps-deakin-drive-the-digital-frontier
70. Mohd, C.K.N.C.K., Shahbodin, F.: Personalized learning environment (PLE) experience in the twenty-first century: review of the literature. In: Abraham, A., Muda, A.K., Choo, Y.-H. (eds.) Pattern Analysis, Intelligent Security and the Internet of Things. AISC, vol. 355, pp. 179–192. Springer, Cham (2015). https://doi.org/10.1007/978-3-319-17398-6_17
71. Cui, W., Xue, Z., Thai, K.P.: Performance comparison of an AI-based adaptive learning system in China. In: 2018 Chinese Automation Congress (CAC), pp. 3170–3175. IEEE (2018)
72. Sandeen, C.: Integrating MOOCs into traditional higher education: the emerging "MOOC 3.0" era. Change Mag. High. Learn. 45(6), 34–39 (2013)
73. Haddad, H., Chevallet, J.P., Bruandet, M.F.: Relations between terms discovered by association rules. In: 4th European Conference on Principles and Practices of Knowledge Discovery in Databases, PKDD, September 2000
74. Schofield, J.W., Evans-Rhodes, D., Huber, B.R.: Artificial intelligence in the classroom: the impact of a computer-based tutor on teachers and students. Soc. Sci. Comput. Rev. 8(1), 24–41 (1990)
75. Tuomi, I.: The impact of artificial intelligence on learning, teaching, and education. Publications Office of the European Union, Luxembourg (2018)
76. Hinojo-Lucena, F.J., Aznar-Díaz, I., Cáceres-Reche, M.P., Romero-Rodríguez, J.M.: Artificial intelligence in higher education: a bibliometric study on its impact in the scientific literature. Educ. Sci. 9(1), 51 (2019)
77. Williams, R., Park, H.W., Breazeal, C.: A is for artificial intelligence: the impact of artificial intelligence activities on young children's perceptions of robots. In: Proceedings of the 2019 CHI Conference on Human Factors in Computing Systems, pp. 1–11, (2019)

78. Deo, R.C., Yaseen, Z.M., Al-Ansari, N., Nguyen-Huy, T., Langlands, T., Galligan, L.: Modern artificial intelligence model development for undergraduate student performance prediction: an investigation on engineering mathematics courses. IEEE Access **8**, 136697–136724 (2020)
79. Mailytica (2020). https://mailytica.com/en/answer-bot/. Accessed 19 June 2020
80. OMQ (2020). https://www.omq.ai/products/reply/. Accessed 19 June 2020
81. Notion (2020). https://notion.ai/. Accessed 19 June 2020
82. Julie (2020). https://www.juliedesk.com/. Accessed 20 June 2020
83. ArtiBot (2020). https://www.artibot.ai/appointmentscheduling. Accessed 20 June 2020
84. Hendrix (2020). https://hendrix.ai/. Accessed 20 June 2020
85. Reddy, T.: How chatbots can help reduce customer service costs by 30%. https://www.ibm.com/blogs/watson/2017/10/how-chatbots-reduce-customer-service-costs-by-30-percent/. Accessed 20 June 2020
86. ActiveChat (2020). https://activechat.ai/?fp_ref=tooltester. Accessed 20 June 2020
87. Respond (2020). https://respond.io/?lmref=yCoaYw. Accessed 20 June 2020
88. ChatBot   (2020).   https://www.chatbot.com/?a=TeV6VODDJ9&utm_source=PP. Accessed 20 June 2020
89. Owoc, M., Pondel, M.: Selection of free software useful in business intelligence. Teaching methodology perspective. In: Mercier-Laurent, E., Boulanger, D. (eds.) Artificial Intelligence for Knowledge Management: 4th IFIP WG 12.6 International Workshop, AI4KM 2016, Held at IJCAI 2016, New York, NY, USA, July 9, 2016, Revised Selected Papers, pp. 93–105. Springer, Cham (2018). https://doi.org/10.1007/978-3-319-92928-6_6
90. Weichbroth, P., Owoc, M., Pleszkun, M.: Web user navigation patterns discovery from WWW server log files. In: 2012 Federated Conference on Computer Science and Information Systems (FedCSIS), pp. 1171–1176. IEEE (2012)
91. Redlarski, K., Weichbroth, P.: Hard lessons learned: delivering usability in IT projects. In: 2016 Federated Conference on Computer Science and Information Systems (FedCSIS), pp. 1379–1382. IEEE (2016)
92. Owoc, M., Weichbroth, P., Żuralski, K.: Towards better understanding of context-aware knowledge transformation. In: 2017 Federated Conference on Computer Science and Information Systems (FedCSIS), pp. 1123–1126. IEEE (2017)
93. Owoc, M.L., Weichbroth, P.: A note on knowledge management education: towards implementing active learning methods. In: Mercier-Laurent, E. (ed.) AI4KM 2018. IAICT, vol. 588, pp. 124–140. Springer, Cham (2020). https://doi.org/10.1007/978-3-030-52903-1_10
94. Ayoub, D.: Artificial intelligence. Unleashing the power of AI for education. MIT Technol. Rev. (2020). https://www.technologyreview.com/2020/03/04/905535/unleashing-the-power-of-ai-for-education/. Accessed 20 June 2020
95. Chiroma, H., et al.: Advances in teaching and learning on Facebook in higher institutions. IEEE Access **5**, 480–500 (2016)
96. Yang, A.M., Li, S.S., Ren, C.H., Liu, H.X., Han, Y., Liu, L.: Situational awareness system in the smart campus. IEEE Access **6**, 63976–63986 (2018)
97. Kim, W.H., Kim, J.H.: Individualized AI tutor based on developmental learning networks. IEEE Access **8**, 27927–27937 (2020)

E-learning as an Extending Tool of Knowledge Management

Katarzyna Hołowińska(✉)

Wroclaw University of Economics, Komandorska 118/120, 53-345 Wroclaw, Poland
katarzyna.holowinska@ue.wroc.pl

Abstract. Acquiring the knowledge by distant education begins to be more and more popular. The main reason of this dynamic development is caused by easy access to the Internet and general IT infrastructure. Nowadays acquiring of knowledge is essential in context of increasing qualifications or education. In such quick technology development traditional forms of learning and teaching are partly inadequate. Consequently teachers and professors look for fresh and new forms of sharing the knowledge with students, but also possibility of verify students abilities. The main goal of the article is to present connection between Knowledge Management and E-learning. The first part describes e-learning concept, the second part highlights Knowledge Management process and the last part describes KM and EL integration.

Keywords: Educational methods · University education · e-learning · Knowledge management

1 Introduction

Undoubtedly one of the main thing which made mankind different from other advanced spices is the fluent ability of learning from each other. In fact intensity of learning process presents also the dynamic of development of modern societies. That is why this is so important to research area of learning and improve the methods of teaching which can have great influence on new generations. Definitely it is easy to noticed that education is area which is often neglected mainly because it is not the space which brings immediate measurable profit. For so many years in schools and on the universities the methods of teaching are almost unchangeable. Despite the technologies in many fields are changing the education and education methods are more less the same. Education supposed to change with the same dynamic as global trends and technologies. The main purpose of this paper is to present that knowledge management can be used in effective way as a e-learning. Organization are more and more interested in knowledge management. The main reason is because KM preserving and systematizing available knowledge. Undoubtedly the Knowledge Management is essential tool for proper functioning of the organization, but it is important to highlight that deployment of KM involves instruments and techniques from broad range of disciplines.

© IFIP International Federation for Information Processing 2021
Published by Springer Nature Switzerland AG 2021
M. L. Owoc and M. Pondel (Eds.): AI4KM 2019, IFIP AICT 599, pp. 59–66, 2021.
https://doi.org/10.1007/978-3-030-85001-2_5

2 The Progress in e-learning Concept

Without doubt the dynamic popularization of the Internet was the biggest reason for such broad availability to resources for both students and teachers. This situation let to share and acquire enormous amount of data and information. E-learning includes creating materials for studying, teaching learners, but also regulating courses within organizations [1]. It is difficult to sum up the idea of e-learning in one definition, mainly because it is constantly changing. Such different perception is caused of specific professional approaches and interests. The development of distance education caused by new technologies and the impact of computer scientists initiated new challenges like how to make integration such technologies in organizations especially in context of lifelong education process. It is possible to emerged four main categories of e-learning definitions [2]:

1) Technology driven which contains technological context of e-learning as a key topic e.g.: "E-learning is the use of electronic media for a variety of learning purposes that range from add-on functions in conventional classrooms to full substitution for the face-to-face meetings by online encounters" (Guri-Rosenblit 2005)"; "E-learning is the use of technology to deliver learning and training programs" (E-learning portal 2009).

2) Delivery system driven which focuses on access to knowledge and the access to resources rather than some achievements e.g.: "E-learning is an on-line education defined as the self-paced or real-time delivery of training and education over the internet to an end-user device" (Lee and Lee 2006)"; "E-learning is the delivery of education (all activities relevant to instructing, teaching, and learning) through various electronic media" (Koohang and Harman 2005)."

3) Communication oriented which includes more interactions aspects like communication and collaboration tools e.g.: "E-learning is education that uses practice communication systems as an environment for communication, the exchange of information and interaction between students and instructors" (Bermejo 2005)"; E-learning is defined as learning facilitated by the use of digital tools and content that involves some form of interactivity, which may include online interaction between the learner and their teacher or peers" (Ministry of Communication and Technology of New Zealand 2008)"

4) Educational-Paradigm driven which consider e-learning as a new proposition of learning and as a development of previous educational paradigm e.g.: "E-learning is a broad combination of processes, content, and infrastructure to use computers and networks to scale and/or improve one or more significant parts of a learning value chain, including management and delivery" (Aldrich 2005).; "E-learning is defined as information and communication technologies used to support students to improve their learning" (Ellis et al. 2009).

This variety definitions present how comprehensive and complex is the idea of e-learning and how broad area is to explore [2] (Fig. 1).

Advantages	Disadvantages
Time flexibility	Limited social interaction
Updated content	All responsibility is on the learner side
Possibility of customization	Development costs
Location flexibility	Reduced individual attention
Fast access to feedback	Technology dependent
Unlimited learning materials	

Fig. 1. E-learning advantages and disadvantages. Source: own elaboration.

2.1 E-learning Nowadays Trends

E-learning functioning in spheres of business and society for several decades and for sure the trend of develop in this field will be strong. The mechanism of delivering knowledge by electronic method seems to be simple but the Information Technology grow and it flexibility empowers variety different approaches and deployments of new learning methods e.g. [3] (Fig. 2):

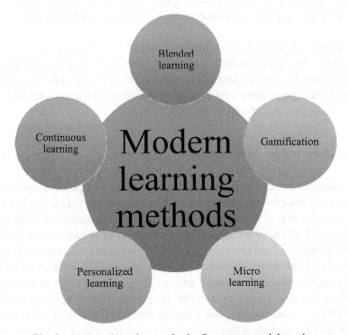

Fig. 2. Modern learning methods. Source: own elaboration.

1) Blended learning- can be described as a process of mixing two or more methods of teaching like, job tasks pedagogical methodology, instructional technologies and web-based technologies. Blended learning combines traditional teaching methods with digital teaching techniques which complement each other depending on the course needs.

2) Gamification is the process of expending e-learning abilities by including game elements, which involves people in commerce and education sectors. The most demanding part of gamification process is creating the player experience which can be divided into creating a gaming application and establishing its exercises in logical sets. In this method the main focus is to design part in such way that the learner achieve goals quicker. Such attitude to learning can be useful especially to build skills, mainly because it gives chance to practice and gets feedback. At the same time it is engaging, fun and satisfying for the user.

3) Micro learning is the learning when there is short and limited time and the material to learn is simple and small, the educational program is divided in parts of modules, the process is repeated and synchronous, used medium is traditional or e-medium, the method is designed for classroom or corporate.

4) Personalized learning offers chance for a user to be a part of creating the content but also the structures of the learning service, in this case user doesn't rely on provided service but have real influence on learning offers.

5) Continuous learning can be described as a constant pursuit for knowledge and skill for own or career goals. This trend can be perceived as a extension and help to traditional education. It is possible to specify 3 principles of continuous learning: learner centrality, equality of opportunity, high quality and relevance.

Definitely the distant learning is very convenient but it seems there is not possible in near future to replace completely traditional education. Direct communication and contact between teacher and student is still very important issue. That is why combining both of forms (b-learning) allows much more opportunities for students and teachers to improve the whole process of education.

3 Today Knowledge Management Aspects

Knowledge management can be define in different forms as a process, system, scientific discipline, new philosophy of management. KM can be considered as a action which is needed to get the key of knowledge resources. The foundation of KM was used to individuals but with the time it changed also in context of organizations. With such big amount of information which around us every day, knowledge management is perceived as significant discipline. Peter Drucker whom is considered as a father of KM said, that the knowledge is the essential resource and not only in field of economic strength but also in a context of nation's military strength. He pointed that there is a necessity to work on the knowledge in contexts of quality and productivity. Certainly nowadays the key resource for the organizations is the collective knowledge which is in deep awareness of all levels in organizational environment like employees, clients or vendors. Identification how to organize knowledge in enterprises gives many profits like [4]:

- developing important business competences,
- increasing level of innovation,
- empowering workers,
- creating high quality products to the market,
- improving time cycles and decision making,
- building strong competitive ad-vantage.

The Institute of system production and projecting technologies in Berlin describe KM as a methods, instruments and tools which effects the progress of core business processes linked to the knowledge which means making distribution and storage of knowledge simultaneously by using the definition of knowledge goals and identification of the knowledge on entirely levels and fields in organization. Stewart define KM as a having a knowledge about the knowledge of particular members of the organizations, obtaining this knowledge and organizing to use it to profit [5].

There are many more different definitions of knowledge management but most of them have some common elements. The idea of knowledge management is built on three main processes: creating, sharing and using the knowledge. In those processes the most important in knowledge management systems are [6]:

- technology (Internet, Extranet, Intranet, group work systems), used as a decision support systems or tools created for individual needs;
- systems, tools and methods which measure efficiency of using the knowledge;
- organizational culture which is focused on people which helps in process of sharing the knowledge;

In organizations the element of modern management is the knowledge with support of technologies and adaptation in different fields.

4   Knowledge Management (KM) and E-Learning (EL) Integration

The integration and synergy of Knowledge Management (KM) and E-learning is not very popular topic of research but undoubtedly it is very important area to study. Collaboration is the essence element where people can both study and work together. To make collaboration happen especially in educational organizations there is tendency to implement virtual learning environment well known as an e-learning (EL). The main idea to provide virtual learning environment is to empower users to work together and engage them in process of knowledge sharing and building together knowledge management (KM). It is important to high- light that using only EL is just enable creating the content management system (CMS). In context of collaboration knowledge supposed to be acquired and shared, that is why the KM is the ideal medium for both of this elements [7].

Combining KM which is more focused on organizational perspective and EL which is more individual learning makes perfect collaborative learning environment. Such approach makes knowledge more globalized. To explain link between KM and EL fields, there is need to use terms integration and adaptation in similar meaning. Integration is used in context when both KM and EL are equal, analogous operating disciplines. Term adaptation is used when one domain is based on another, methods and tools from another domain are adapted to improve efficiency [8]. KM tools are fundamental to make major range of EL improvement thanks to extension to broader communities. Integration of KM and EL is necessary tendency in process of self-directed and just in time learning [9].

Creating intensive knowledge growth is possible due to providing collaborative learning environment in organization. EL is concentrated on individual learning rather than collaborative learning. KM maintain the human tacit knowledge codification into physical form in order to learning. EL systems ensure support and develop of users knowledge through design structure of learning contents and intercommunication options. However KMS (Knowledge Management System) deliver knowledge to CMS (Content Management System) to sort and search amenities and also cooperation chances between experts and other users. KM and EL integration processes enable to develop synergy which is essential in improving the formation of new knowledge but also the creation of learning processes [10].

Definitely integration of KM and EL is an inevitable tendency in processes of self-directed and just in time learning but also significant support in process of sharing the knowledge in organizations. KM processes which take part in context of learning are [7] (Fig. 3):

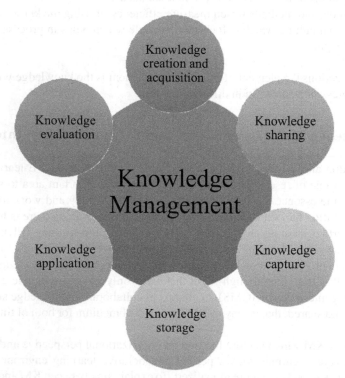

Fig. 3. Knowledge Management process connected with e-learning. Source: own elaboration.

- Knowledge creation and acquisition, which include increase amount of people with knowledge both individual or groups which practicing to gain the knowledge in form of intangible tacit knowledge;
- Knowledge sharing which include creation of learning process while people are interested in helping each other to grow and gain new knowledge;
- Knowledge capture which is about converting tacit knowledge into explicit;
- Knowledge storage which is knowledge repository which contains databases, documents or reports.
- Knowledge application where created and captured knowledge is used in variety learning contexts;
- Knowledge evaluation which include assessing learners for verifying knowledge which supposed to be relevant and accurate.

5 Conclusions

Today organisations need to learn from own experiences and have tools to collect best practise and have possibilities to learned from other organisations. Definitely the importance of knowledge management is increasing especially because of the connection between knowledge and learning in organisations.

Environment connected with e-learning can be used as an effective medium for knowledge management, in many organizations knowledge management is strongly concentrated on the connection between learning and knowledge. Learning always supposed to combine theory with practice and knowledge with experience [11] such attitude is different from traditional learning but it does'nt mean that traditional learning will be completely insignificant. It seems that now the best solution is still to combine the modern methods with this more traditional.

References

1. Arkorful, V., Abaidoo, N.: The role of e-learning, advantages and disadvantages of its adoption in higher education. Int. J. Instructional Technol. Dist. Learn. **12**(1), 29–42 (2015)
2. Sangrà, A., Vlachopoulos, D., Cabrera, N.: Building an inclusive definition of E-Learning: an approach to the conceptual framework. Int. Rev. Res. Open Dist. Learn. **13**(2), 145–159 (2012)
3. Bezhovski, Z., Poorani, S.: The evolution of E-Learning and new trends. Inf. Knowl. Manage. **6**(3), 50–57 (2016)
4. Oprea, M.: A university knowledge management tool for academic research activity evaluation. Inform. Economică **15**(3), 58 (2011)
5. Becerra-Fernandez, R.S.: Knowledge management: Systems and Processes. Routledge, New York (2015)
6. Mikuła, B., Pietruszka-Ortyl, A., Potocki, A.: Zarządzanie przedsiębiorstwem XXI wieku. Wybrane koncepcje i metody, Difin, Warszawa (2002)
7. Pattnayak, J. Pattnaik, S. Priyaranjan, Dash, P.: Knowledge management in E-Learning a critical analysis. Int. J. Eng. Comput. Sci. **6**, 21528–21533. ISSN: 2319-7242 (2017)
8. Judrups, J.: Analysis of knowledge management and E-Learning integration models. ICTE Reg. Dev. Procedia Comput. Sci. **43**, 154–162 (2014)

9. Khdour, T., Salem, S.: The effects of integrating management with E-Learning. In: Proceedings of 2014 Zone 1 Conference of the American Society for Engineering Education (ASEE Zone 1) (2014)
10. Yilmaz, Y.: Knowledge management in E-Learning practices. TOJET Turkish Online J. Educ. Technol. **11**(2), 150–155 (2012)
11. Choenni, Walker, Bakker, Baets1 E-learning as a Vehicle for Knowledge Management, Nyenrode University
12. Marciniak, K., Owoc, M.L.: Knowledge management as foundation of smart university. In: Ganzha, M., Maciaszek, L.A., Paprzycki, M. (eds.) Federated Conference on Computer Science and Information Systems - FedCSIS 2013, Kraków, Poland, 8–11 September 2013, Proceedings (2013)
13. Mercier-Laurent, E.: Knowledge Management and Risk Management. In: Federal Conference on Computer Science and Information Systems (2016)
14. Przysucha, Ł: Content management systems based on GNU GPL license as a support of knowledge management in organizations and business. In: Mercier-Laurent, E., Boulanger, D. (eds.) AI4KM 2015. IAICT, vol. 497, pp. 51–65. Springer, Cham (2016). https://doi.org/10.1007/978-3-319-55970-4_4
15. Przysucha, L.: Knowledge management processes in smart city-electronic tools supporting the exchange of information and knowledge among city residents. Int. J. Innov. Manage. Technol. **10**(4), 155–160 (2019)
16. Owoc, M., Weichbroth, P.: Validation model for discovered web user navigation patterns. In: Mercier-Laurent, E., Boulanger, D. (eds.) AI4KM 2012. IAICT, vol. 422, pp. 38–52. Springer, Heidelberg (2014). https://doi.org/10.1007/978-3-642-54897-0_3

Internet of Things as a Significant Factor of Innovations in an Intelligent Organization

Piotr Domagała (✉) (iD)

Wroclaw University of Economics, Komandorska 118/120, 53-345 Wrocław, Poland
piotr.domagala@ue.wroc.pl

Abstract. The network of things communicating not only with people, but communicating with each other generate a vast number of data called Big Data. Internet of Things (IoT) will open huge data streams of real-time action and response. Artificial Intelligence (AI) will help companies tap archival as well as fresh data insights for real-time, rapid-response decisions. The author shows the evolution of Knowledge Management in the organization at the beginning. In the next part, the author presents SMAC, IoT and AI technologies as a background of an intelligent organization. All considerations lead to presentation of modern business models built on a synergy between AI and IoT.

Keywords: Knowledge management · Intelligent organization · Internet of Things · Artificial Intelligence · Digital transformation · Business model

1 Introduction

The role of information and communication technologies (ICT) is huge. Increasing usage of mobile devices and social media, the development of technical solutions based on network services and the progressing digitization are shaping the new socio-economic landscape. Until now, IT solutions have been used mainly to increase the effectiveness of an organization's operations by reducing costs and improving processes. Digitization and computerization were treated functionally as separate elements of company operations. Modern solutions, i.e. the Internet of Things, cloud computing or Big Data, are treated as the main factors of change. They affect not only savings and improvements, but also new sources of income and ways of operating the organization. These horizontal changes caused by new technological solutions are called the digital transformation of the organization. Their effects include using new business models, searching for new sources of profits, innovations and ways of competing, improving the enterprise management process and applying new performance measures.

The author also notices changes in the Knowledge Management process in the organization as a result of technological progress what lead to evolution in this area of the enterprise. Data, information and knowledge are treated as elements determining the

M. L. Owoc and M. Pondel (Eds.): AI4KM 2019, IFIP AICT 599, pp. 67–79, 2021.
https://doi.org/10.1007/978-3-030-85001-2_6

success of enterprises and, at the same time as factors that significantly affect the creation of competitive advantage by increasing the attractiveness and competitiveness of the company. Modern enterprises wishing to achieve a certain position on the market need to adapt to dynamically changing environment. Traditional production factors: land, labor, capital, are losing importance for the key resource that knowledge is in the creative functioning.

The first section of this paper elaborates increasing role of Knowledge Management and the essence of intelligent organization concept. Next covers the idea of Internet of Things (IoT) – digital transformation and evolution of the Internet, main IoT perspectives and the reasons for the success of this technology as a technological background of modern organization. In the third part of the chapter the author presents the power of IoT and AI synergy and its benefits for KM process.

2   Growing Role of Knowledge Management in Modern Organization

2.1   Knowledge Management in Modern Enterprise

Data, information and knowledge are treated as elements determining the success of enterprises and, at the same time, as factors that significantly affect on the competitive advantage by increasing the attractiveness and competitiveness of the company [1].

According to the theory of knowledge-based organizations, knowledge by itself does not create a competitive advantage, and it is achieved through its application and integration with the company's business processes [2]. The author also emphasizes that simply providing knowledge is not a sufficient condition for its application. In practice, a more serious problem is the lack of use of knowledge when a company or individuals have it. It is a common problem especially when we consider rapid technology evolution and emergence of new, unstructured kind knowledge e.g. from delivered by Internet of Things.

Knowledge Management (KM) is, in part, an attempt of the best possible use of knowledge, which is available in organization, creation of new knowledge and growth of knowledge understands [3].

Knowledge as a resource needs to be managed in appropriate way what leads to KM development and dissemination of intelligent organization concept.

2.2   Intelligent Organization Concept

Intelligent organization is assumed that it is an organization bases its philosophy on Knowledge Management. This term has become so popular due to the rapid development of ICT, dynamically changing economic environment and increased market competitiveness. We can consider organization as intelligent when it is a learning organization with the ability to create, acquire knowledge, organize, share it and use it to increase efficiency and competitiveness on the global market [4].

The organization is treated as a complex organism, based on existing structures and implemented processes with a particular definition of the role of knowledge. Thanks to the knowledge and appropriate tools, all organizational components and staff are able to skillfully cooperate in achieving specific goals. The organization functions as a well-performing body in a competitive environment [5].

The growing volume of information used in the intelligent organization goes hand in hand with the increase of its meaning and can be considered as a valuable resource for the organization. Main resources of knowledge are data about clients, products, processes, environment, etc. in a formalized form (documents, databases) and non-codified (knowledge of employees). Knowledge becomes treated as resource itself. Resource equals land, labor, money etc. As the author shows at the picture below, growing number of usable data, knowledge treated as a valuable resource for business and KM development determine engine of modern, intelligent organization (Fig. 1).

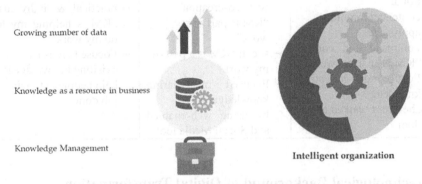

Growing number of data

Knowledge as a resource in business

Knowledge Management

Intelligent organization

Fig. 1. The idea of intelligent organization.

Dynamic changes in the environment force changes in KM strategy and philosophy. KM is no longer an extra work to do. It is helpful to do our work in a real time (Table 1).

It would not be possible without the continuous development of ICT technologies. The author, in the next part of the paper, focuses on the important role of IoT technology in the evolution of KM.

Table 1. Evolution and development of knowledge management.

KM 1.0	KM 2.0	KM 3.0
Collecting	**Sharing**	**Using**
techno-centric approach	people-centric approach	productivity-centric approach
— traditional organizational content/community approaches — command and control "KM is an extra work" — Focused on collecting knowledge „before it walked at the door"	— enriched with social media and ecosystem wide co-creation "KM is part of my work" — social "KM is a part of my work" — Focused on sharing knowledge by using web-enabled and Social Media tools	— KM augmented with AI — practical & individual „KM is helping my to do my work" — Focused on using exisiting knowledge to help people get their job done

3 Technological Background of Digital Transformation

3.1 Digital Transformation

The Internet of Things is currently one of the most-discussed topics in the context of the impact of modern information technology on the management and functioning of an organization. According to many authors, no topic has ever been so popular in scientific and post-scientific works. This may be result of its wide application in business, management, marketing and applies to almost every industry [6].

Organizations are facing new challenges, but for most of them digital transformation is one of the foundations for maintaining its position and further market expansion.

Digital transformation means changing the approach to the client and a comprehensive process of transitioning the organization to new ways of functioning using the latest IoT and SMAC digital technologies (social, mobile, analytics, cloud). The table below presents main benefits of each of these solutions (Table 2).

The author points out that the key to success in the application of SMAC is the combination of the four technologies mentioned above, which by communicating with each other, allow for synergy. None of the four technologies are able to effect themselves. Only close cooperation allows and building a competitive advantage.

Table 2. SMAC foundations.

Social	– Better interaction between business and clients – Faster response to problem and building a knowledge base based on users preferences and behaviors – Employees can share information faster and easier, which speeds up problem solving (collective intelligence)
Mobile	– Increase reach of companies to customers (multi-channel distribution) – Entrepreneurs must develop their internet marketing channels and share mobile channels – The offer for mobile devices is the basis to gain and maintain a high market position
Analytics	– Understanding behavior and preferences of customers by using advanced algorithms and analytical tools (Big Data). – Making correct decisions based on current and aggregated information
Cloud	– Lowering ICT costs – Breaking down geographical barriers – Access to data anywhere, anytime The cloud combines all SMAC elements together

Digital transformation means horizontal changes caused by a new wave of technological solutions. The expression of these changes are, among others new business models, seeking new sources of profit, innovations and ways of competing, improving operational management of an enterprise, implementing new methods of talent management, and applying new measures of effectiveness. At the same time, the customer is being transformed and becomes a co-creator of values [7] (Fig. 2).

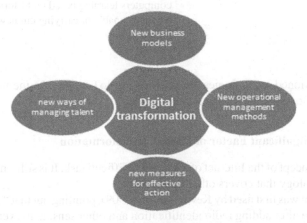

Fig. 2. Dimensions of digital transformation.

The digital transforamtion would not be possible without new technologies. The author want to point out a few important solutions determining this process in the table below (Table 3).

Table 3. Solutions determining digital transformation.

Sensor systems	Devices that capture signals from the surrounding environment. Cooperating within larger networks with smart devices and applications. The costs of using them decrease over time
RFID/NFC/Beacons	Tags, labels, cards capable of exchanging data with readers, using radio-based communication. Solutions introducing a number of facilities for clients for the benefit of enterprises, e.g. tracking consumer activity, improvements in logistics
Inter-machine communication	Automation of machine work allows to optimize the production process and reduce maintenance costs
Robotics	Practical solutions used include by car manufacturers and in the logistics industry
Virtual and augmented reality	Solutions based on AI/AR allow to eliminate or reduce significantly maintenance costs, costs of designing and modeling new solutions offered to consumers. Huge potential in the entertainment, marketing and healthcare industries
Artificial Intelligence/cognitive data processing/machine and deep learning	Machine and deep learning (computers learn on the basis of an advanced neural network) make computers learning based on historical data become capable of carrying out new tasks with high accuracy

All of mentioned technologies are parts of the IoT engine. In the next part of the chapter the author explains its phenomenon.

3.2 IoT as a Significant Factor of Digital Transformation

Defining the concept of the Internet of Things is a difficult task. It is still a new, constantly evolving technology that covers other new fields.

This concept was first used by Kevin Ashton (2009), pointing out that "The Internet of Things can arise after adding radio identification and other sensors to everyday objects" [8]. The concept of the Internet of Things can also be referred to the ideas of Nikolas Tesla, who 100 years ago pointed out that when wireless technologies will be fully developed, the Earth will transform into one big brain, and the devices that create its innervation will be very easy compared to the current phone [9].

   M. Porter and J. Heppelman define the Internet of Things, referring to the techno-logical sphere, indicating that they are intelligent products with Internet access, which consist of:

– physical, mechanical and electrical components,
– intelligent components - sensors, processors, data carriers, control mechanisms, software, operating systems,
– elements enabling communication, e.g. ports, antennas, data transmission protocols, communication systems.

   A lot definitions, such as mentioned above, is strictly connected with technolog-ical aspects of functioning. The author notes that IoT can be considered in the other dimensions. IoT from different perspectives can be considered as [10]:

– business ecosystem,
– Internet of Everything,
– IoT (Gartner).

   From a business perspective, IoT can be seen as a collection of services using objects that collect and process information (interactions), networked and ensure interoperability and synergy of applications (Fig. 3).

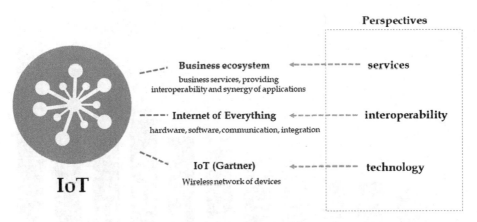

Fig. 3. IoT dimensions.

   Combining Internet of Things products/services allows a better understanding of the consumer, the environment, products and processes, identifying significant events and responding for immediate optimization or more accurate personalization.

The architectural perspective (Internet as Everything) is a concept that enables the cooperation of various ICT systems that support various domain applications and is based on four layers:

- Equipment - sensors, actuators, controllers, smartphones, computers that are able to communicate and process data without human involvement or limited interaction with it.
- Communication - telecommunications infrastructure and telecommunication network, working on any data transmission standards (Internet)
- Software - IT systems for IoT devices and software for data exchange, processing, system management and security.
- Integration - sets of defined IT services ensuring software interoperability at all levels of architecture.

Gartner's definition has been presented in the paragraph above.

All perspectives show how huge potential is generated by IoT. Also the numbers confirm this fact. As it presented at the picture below, the number of devices that make up the Internet of Things is still growing (Fig. 4).

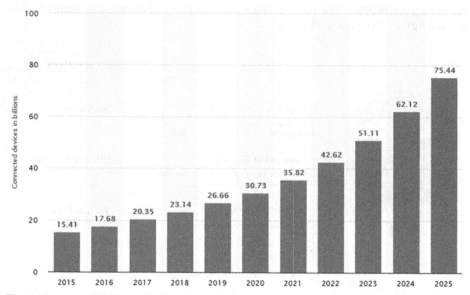

Fig. 4. Internet of Things (IoT) connected devices installed base worldwide between 2015 and 2025. Source: https://www.statista.com/statistics/471264/iot-number-of-connected-devices-worldwide/, last accessed 2020/04/21.

Experts predict rapid growth on the IoT market. In the years 2015 to 2025, the number of devices connected to the Internet of Things is predicted to be almost five times higher. This is a huge potential for business due to the amount of generated data.

Three features distinguish IoT from other technologies. They are context, ubiquity and optimization. Objects provide data, e.g. in terms of physical condition, location, or weather conditions, by using M2M (machine to machine) interaction. The ubiquity is illustrated by the fact that today there are more such intelligent things than their users connected to the network. Optimization comes down to so-called expression of functionality, which brings every object based on built intelligence and resulting new synergistic properties. Therefore, the real value of IoT is not merely having data, but combining business processes with deliveries, orders and production, or the work schedule being implemented [11].

4   Internet of Things and Artifical Intelligence – Opportunities for KM and Innovations in Business

4.1   Why IoT Needs AI

Artificial Intelligence (AI) and the Internet of Things (IoT) are terms that project futuristic, sci-fi, imagery; both have been identified as drivers of business disruption. But in fact they are more real today than any time in the past. However in order for companies to realize the full potential of IoT, they need to combine IoT with rapidly-advancing Artificial Intelligence (AI) technologies, which enable 'smart machines' to simulate intelligent behavior and make well-informed decisions with little or no human intervention.

AI, on the other hand, is the engine or the "brain" that will enable analytics and decision making from the data collected by IoT. In other words, IoT collects the data and AI processes this data in order to make sense of it. You can see these systems working together at a personal level in devices like fitness trackers and Google Home, Amazon's Alexa, and Apple's Siri.

With more connected devices comes more data that has the potential to provide amazing insights for businesses but presents a new challenge for how to analyse it all. Collecting this data benefits no one unless there is a way to understand it all. This is where AI comes in. Making sense of huge amounts of data is a perfect application for pure AI.

By applying the analytic capabilities of AI to data collected by IoT, companies can identify and understand patterns and make more informed decisions. This leads to a variety of benefits for both consumers and companies such as proactive intervention, intelligent automation and highly personalised experiences. It also enables us to find ways for connected devices to work better together and make these systems easier to use.

This, in turn, leads to even higher adoption rates. That's exactly why we need to improve the speed and accuracy of data analysis with AI in order to see IoT live up to its promise. Collecting data is one thing, but sorting, analyzing, and making sense of that data is a completely different thing. This is why essential to develop faster and more accurate AIs in order to keep up with the sheer volume of data being collected as IoT starts to penetrate almost all aspects of our lives [12].

Security, energy adoption, building management, smart homes and cities, telemedicine, embedded mobile, agriculture automation, vehicle, person & pet controlling and everyday things – these are only a few examples of IoT usage in everyday life (Fig. 5).

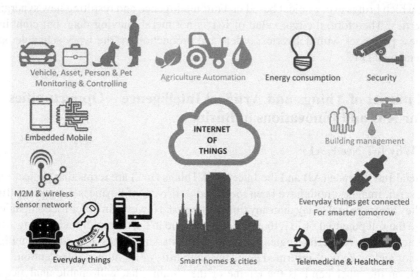

Vehicle, Asset, Person & Pet Monitoring & Controlling

Agriculture Automation

Energy consumption

Security

Embedded Mobile

INTERNET OF THINGS

Building management

M2M & wireless Sensor network

Everyday things get connected For smarter tomorrow

Everyday things

Smart homes & cities

Telemedicine & Healthcare

Fig. 5. IoT in everyday life. Source: https://www.supinfo.com/articles/single/4235-internet-of-things, last accessed: 2019/06/06.

The author intentionally omitted aspects of running an organization. They will be presented in the next part.

4.2   Business Models – Unlocking Value from Technology

As it was mentioned at the beginning of the chapter, rapid digital revolution forces organization to constant changes. Changes in their philosophy and way of doing business. New technologies allow to reach a wider group of customers through new channels (mobile devices), obtain from them data on their preferences, thanks to which the offered products are closely tailored to their needs.

A modern value chain should start with the customer. The customer is here the first link, the driving force that touches all links, needs and priorities [13]. Data on the new structure requires tools that will allow you to find out what customers need and understand the various sources of customer intelligence, so as to use those that will allow them to get closer to them [14].

New opportunities resulting from IoT solutions translate into business models that are the essence of innovation in these systems. The following solutions can be indicated here [15] (Table 4):

Table 4. Business models determined by IoT

Model	Specification/Example
Anything as a service	Observed migration processes from the purchase of a product by the customer to one in which the producer infringes the ownership of it, while the consumer uses it, paying only for its real use. e.g.: AI as a service
New form of outsourcing (cloud computing)	Remote monitoring of real estate, airports or hotel chains
Big data analytics	Forecasting consumer traffic based on geolocation data downloaded from smartphones
Intelligent products	Products that are a source of additional benefits for the customer, e.g. by remote monitoring and optimizing the use of construction machinery and equipment Eg. Caterpillar machines and construction equipment equipped with sensors to track machines condition in real-time
Behavioral profiling	In the scope of Progressive insurance company setting rates, based on analyzing the vehicle driver's driving style on the basis of mounted teelmetric devices
Additional services related to physical products	Rollce-Roys offers airlines a Power-by-Hour engine model. Users pay for the time of real use of the engine instead of incurring one-off costs associated with its purchase and additional costs associated with its servicing
Hybrid solutions	Solutions that compromise between Product-as-a-Service models and traditional customer purchasing. Their sale can be combined with various service contracts based on remote monitoring of equipment functioning
IoT platforms	Apple HomeKit systems that allow home devices from various manufacturers to be controlled via a smartphone application

The business models presented in table above can translate into organizational changes. They may result primarily from the need for a new approach to data management aspects, creating new solutions related to the products and services offered, and a new approach to customer relationship management. This may mean the need to create new functional departments in organizations dealing with, for example, managing large amounts of data collected from the IoT (undifiend data organization) ecosystem and analyzing them [16].

An example of an innovative IoT business model due to the possibility of full insight into the way users use products is the Rolls-Royce sales model. This means offering products in the form of services, which translates into changes in the activities of sales and marketing departments.

5 Summary

The spread of the Internet of Things means that solutions in this field become the norm, an integral part of every product. Sensors, processors and their specialized software are integrated into their functionality and combined with advanced data analytics. This leads in a straight line to the creation of new and improved products (services), which allows a noticeable jump in economic efficiency.

Digital transformation significantly changes the approach to the basic macroeconomic principles of market mechanisms. ICT solutions based on SMAC systems are playing an increasingly important role. This allows making fundamental structural changes by combining new models with the decomposition of value sources into digital components that, when reconfigured, translate into the emergence of new variations of business models.

This leads to the need for constant changes in the organization. Such activities include the creation of new functional departments dealing with data management in an organization headed by a person located at the level of top management (Chief Data Officer). It may also be necessary to create an organizational unit that integrates co-operation between ICT, R&D and production departments. This mean necessary changes in the organizational culture in terms of accepting decision-making based on business analytics (data-driven decision making), or sharing information. These are the essential elements of Knowledge Management in an intelligent organization.

The coming years will be marked by the growing importance of IoT-based solutions. The development of analytics is a key direction for IoT transformations, because it will increase the intelligence range of devices and systems. Machine learning processes will make it possible to reduce human involvement in problems that are not particularly complicated. The future of IoT involves creating better and better tools to support people and sometimes replace them during simple analyzes. Artificial Intelligence and prediction algorithms will allow you to eliminate downtime associated with failures, and intelligent products will be better adapted to the needs of consumers.

Each enterprise is a kind of combination of resources and/or possibilities of acquiring them, skills, information and knowledge, dermining a specific level of competence in the desired market position.

In the past, the strategy was to achieve lasting competitive advantage. The idea was to find something that could be done better than other companies in the industry. In the current, changing environment, companies need a more adaptive approach, so they can constantly improve strategy and goals. Instead of achieving excellence in one, enterprises are deepening their competences in new and diversified areas, focusing on the customer.

To make it possible organizations need to launch new business approaches strictly connected with innovative Knowledge Management based on IoT & AI solutions.

References

1. Jashapara, A.: Knowledge Management. An Integrated Approach. Pearson Education Limited, London (2004)
2. Kowalczyk, A., Nogalski, B.: Zarządzanie wiedzą. Koncepcje i narzędzia. Difin, Warszawa (2007)
3. Przysucha, Ł: Knowledge management in corporations – synergy between people and technology. Barriers and benefits of implementation. In: Mercier-Laurent, E., Boulanger, D. (eds.) AI4KM 2017. IAICT, vol. 571, pp. 1–11. Springer, Cham (2019). https://doi.org/10.1007/978-3-030-29904-0_1
4. Domagała, P.: Internet of things and big data technologies as an opportunity for organizations based on knowledge management. In: Proceedings of 2019 IEEE 10th International Conference on Mechanical and Intelligent Manufacturing Technologies (ICMIMT 2019), pp. 199–203. IEEE Press, Cape Town (2019)
5. Senge, P.M.: The Fifth Discipline. The Art and Practice of the Learning Organisation. Random House Business Books, London (2006)
6. Atzori, L., Iera, A., Morabito, G.: Understanding the Internet of Things: definition, potentials and societal role of a fast evolving paradigm. Ad Hoc Netw. (56), 4 (2017)
7. Mazurek, G., Tkaczyk, J.: The impact of the Digital World on Management and Marketing. Poltex, Warszawa (2016)
8. Ashton, K.: That "Internet of Things" thing. RFID J. **22**(7), 97–114 (2009)
9. Tesla, A.: Teleautomation, USA (1926)
10. Digital Poland Homepage. https://www.digitalpoland.org/assets/publications/iot-w-polskiej-gospodarce/iot-w-polskiej-gospodarce-raport.pdf. Accessed 06 June 2019
11. Gajewski, J., Paprocki, W., Pieriegud, J.: Cyfryzacja polskiej gospodarki I społeczeństwa – szanse I wyzwania dla sektorów infrastrukturalnych. Instytut Badań nad Gospodarką Rynkową, Gdańsk (2016)
12. BBVA OpenMind Homepage. https://www.bbvaopenmind.com/en/technology/digital-world/why-iot-needs-ai/. Accessed 06 June 2019
13. Janasz, W., Kozioł-Nadolna, K.: Innowacje w organizacji. PWE, Warszawa (2011)
14. Customer Intelligence: What It Is and Why It's Important. https://www.cmnty.com/blog/customer-intelligence/. Accessed 06 June 2019
15. Heppelman, J., Porter, M.: How Smart, Connected products are Transforming Companies. Harvard Bus. Rev. 96–106 (2015)
16. Kaczorowska-Spychalska, D., Sułkowski, Ł.: Internet of Things. Nowy Paradygmat Rynku., pp. 66–77, Difin, Warszawa (2018)

Semantics Visualization as a User Interface in Business Information Searching

Helena Dudycz[✉] [iD]

Wrocław University of Economics and Business, Wrocław, Poland
helena.dudycz@ue.wroc.pl

Abstract. The article sets out to present conclusions from the conducted research into semantic network visualization as a user interface applied for the purpose of searching for business information. The article describes the results of the research comprising literature analysis as well as the validation of prototypes developed in Protégé. Based on the analysis of publications covering the latest research, four areas of research into semantic network visualization were identified, i.e. the development of new software, the application of techniques, technologies, and solutions making it possible to perform various operations concerning the semantic network visualization view, the verification of the use of various graphic designations, as well as users' validation of interactive semantic network visualization. For each area, the main directions of research are specified, along with an indication of publications that describe them. Furthermore, the article provides conclusions from the validation of prototypes of ontologies for the area of users' (experts') analysis of economic and financial indicators using semantic network visualization. The research in question allowed the identification of three potential problems related to the use of semantic network visualization as a visual interface in searching for economic information.

Keyword: Semantic visualization · Interface · Visual interface · Knowledge visualization · Ontology

1 Introduction

Visualization is currently treated as one of the basic solutions for the presentation of both information and knowledge obtained from systems supporting enterprise management. Particular attention is paid to graphic methods enabling knowledge visualization. One of them is the semantic network, which can present an ontology containing knowledge pertaining to a specific field. Along with the visualization of information and the visualization of knowledge, the concept of Semantics Visualization has appeared, describing technologies associated with ontology and visualizing semantic structures search [1–3]. The visualization of semantic searches is essential, as it allows users to more easily notice and understand various semantic and structural dependencies between topics. Using semantic network visualization, the user should be able to interactively select the elements of interest to them, i.e. concepts and relationships between them. There is an

© IFIP International Federation for Information Processing 2021
Published by Springer Nature Switzerland AG 2021
M. L. Owoc and M. Pondel (Eds.): AI4KM 2019, IFIP AICT 599, pp. 80–90, 2021.
https://doi.org/10.1007/978-3-030-85001-2_7

increasing focus on developing methods and tools to graphically visualize ontologies, which could be an effective representation of ontologies in order to fully understand the structures [4, 5]. The issues of searching for information using semantic networks, based on a created ontology for a selected field, is the subject of numerous studies and concerns various domains [6–10].

Semantic visualization can play a dual role. First of all, as a visual, interactive method for presenting knowledge belonging to a given domain. Secondly, as a visual, interactive interface allowing the user's active involvement in the process of searching for unique information. The combination of data visualization in the shape of a semantic network and personalized navigation can become an effective and efficient tool for carrying out a variety of business information analyses [11]. This is possible on condition that the semantic network visualization applied is a useful and easy interface for users. This statement became a premise for undertaking the research.

This article aims to present the conclusions of the conducted research dedicated to semantic network visualization as a user interface applied in searching for business information. The research covers two areas. The first one covers an analysis of the literature describing the latest research into the application of semantic network visualization as a visual interface. The second one consists in the validation of ontology prototypes for the area of users' (experts') analysis of economic and financial indicators using semantic network visualization. The structure of the article is as follows. The next section briefly discusses visualization, ontology, and semantics visualization. The following section presents the conclusions from the research conducted into literature as well as experts' tests of prototypes created with the Protégé software. The article ends with a summary.

2 Theoretical Background

There are numerous definitions of visualization in the literature. Among the many of them, due to the subject of this article, the following may be mentioned. Visualization is the process of representing data as a visual image [12], offering "a link between the human eye and the computer, helping to identify patterns and to extract insights from large amounts of information" [13, p. 139]. Visualization is defined also as "the use of computer-supported, interactive, visual representations of abstract data to amplify cognition" [14, p. 477]. Interactive visualization actively includes the user in the process of finding information, enabling him or her to build more accurate queries for a specific set of data [15]. Particular attention is paid to the role of visualization, which is multifaceted and enables interactive visual search for information [16, 17].

Visualization has also begun to be interpreted not only as a way of transmitting information by means of graphic elements, but also as a method of data set exploration, helping the user to identify patterns, correlations, etc. [13], or as a method of knowledge representation aiming to improve knowledge transfer [18] between two or more people [19]. Visualization of knowledge is "an essential element of knowledge management and aims to support the process of knowledge transfer and creation using visualization techniques" [20]. Knowledge visualization methods include the following: the knowledge map, hierarchical semantic visualization, relational semantic visualization, and semantic visualization based on entities (discussed in [20]).

One of the ideas of collecting and searching for data is the semantic network, which besides the data itself contains also information on relations between them [21]. It is a directed or undirected graph, where the vertices represent concepts while the edges represent relations between the concepts. The graph's pathways can reflect implicit knowledge [7, 20]. Formalized domain knowledge using created ontologies forms the basis of the semantic network. Ontology describes "the concepts and relationships in an area of knowledge using a logic-based language and have a related graphical representation" [4]. A wide review of ontology is presented in [22]. Ontology is a model describing a given field in a formalized manner, reproducing knowledge with the use of identified notions and links existing between them including mutual relations, cause-effect relationships, and properties. In recent years, researchers have developed a variety of techniques to visually present ontologies [23–26]; various ontology visualization tools are presented in [5, 27, 28]. Ontology-driven applications are already used in knowledge management, intelligent integration of information resources, commerce etc. (see for example [4, 7]). In the literature, the visualization of ontologies using a semantic network began to be referred to as Semantics Visualization [1–3]. Information search using a semantic network is the subject of many studies and the concern of various fields [29–34].

Human interaction with semantic visualization plays an important role in acquiring knowledge [2]. The basic assumption of navigation in the visualization of a semantic network is that it should allow the user to look at fine-detail (focused) information and full-system context simultaneously, thereby presenting an overview of the whole knowledge structure [3]. In this interactive process, the user can concentrate on the interesting data elements by filtering uninteresting data, and focusing (zooming in) on the interesting elements, until finally, details are available for an interesting subset of the analyzed elements. Each action performed (choice of a node, mouse click on a node, etc.) expresses knowledge specific to the user of this application [20]. In order for the user to easily move from the global view to the detailed view by interacting with the visualization interface, many approaches have been developed, for example: "overview + details" and "focus + context". This method of searching for information by means of a semantic network meets the basic principle of visualization proposed by Shneiderman (overview first, zoom and filter, then details on demand) [35].

3 Description of the Research

3.1 Research Questions

The conclusions presented in this article stem from the research into the use of semantic network visualization as an interface in searching for business information. The research undertaken is expected to provide answers to the following questions:

- What research work is being carried out with respect to the application of semantic network visualization in users' searching for information?
- Can semantic network visualization be a friendly interface for users (experts) seeking to gain economic knowledge?

The next section presents the conclusions resulting from the research conducted into the literature on the application of semantic visualization as a visual interface employed for the purpose of searching for information. Sect. 3.3 presents the most important conclusions from the validation of prototypes created in Protégé with the participation of experts.

3.2 Results of the Literature Research

The research was carried out based on the approach described in [36]. The study aimed to identify the most recent research into the application of interactive semantic network visualization for the purpose of users' searching for information. Therefore, the Google Scholar search engine was chosen, which allows obtaining information about the latest publications from various databases. Due to the adopted criterion according to which the subject of examination has to be the latest research, the dates for publications to be considered were set from 2010 to 2019.

First, a Google Scholar search was conducted for the terms "Semantic Network Visualization" + "interface" and "Semantic web Visualization" + "interface". As a result of setting the keywords in this way, in either set, the result was fewer than forty indications, of which just under than ten remained after the preliminary analysis. However, in order not to omit important publications pertaining to this area, another search was conducted for the combination of the following terms: "Semantic Visualization" + "interface". As a result without time limits 500 publications were received, while in 2010–2019 there were 362. After a preliminary analysis, 49 out of 362 were chosen. After another analysis of publications and the application of the snowballing technique, 13 publications related to the research question were received.

The analysis of the research described in the publications obtained allowed the identification of four areas. The first of these concerns the development of software for the visualization of semantic networks as an interactive tool applied by users to search for information or knowledge. Special attention should be paid to the development of software for the semantic search visualization, an import research area in the context of semantic visualization. A far as this area is concerned, the following software under development should be mentioned:

- Knowledge cockpit with many tools for visualizing semantic information [37];
- TopicViz [38];
- SemaZoom [39];
- SemaTime [40];
- NavigOWL (a plug-in for Protégé) [5];
- MUCK [41];
- ONTOLIS [4];
- MCVGraphViz [20].

The second area concerns techniques, technologies, and solutions enabling the user to modify the view of semantic network visualization. The visual interface should allow navigation between topics in a highly interactive manner. Interesting nodes can be put in the foreground by zooming, panning, and rotating. For instance, users should be able to hide irrelevant branches of the tree or expand interesting ones as well as to perform "overview + details" and "focus + context" Research into this area is described in the following publications:

- manipulating the visualization by adding, rearranging, or removing topics [3, 5, 37, 39, 40];
- applying different colours to the graph elements (i.e. nodes and lines) [3, 5, 39, 42];
- viewing the graph as a whole or obtaining a partial view by disabling certain nodes and edges [3, 5, 20, 37, 39, 41, 42];
- applying semantics-based filtration [3, 5, 20, 37–41];
- creating a system of tooltips to refine the access to the knowledge represented in the model [20].

The third area concerns the graphic designations used. The typically used graphic elements are rectangles, which symbolise terms (nodes), and lines in various colours, which indicate types of connections between these terms. The publication [20] proposes a circle as a node symbol. The diameter of the circle depends on the number of other nodes linked to it, while its colour is defined by the category to which the node belongs. This method of coding may help the user to detect the nodes (terms) in which they are interested in semantic network visualization.

The fourth area is research involving users in the use of visualization of a semantic network for obtaining information. The literature points to various potential problems that can occur in semantic network visualization software, which could be caused by a very considerable number of displayed nodes and lines in the semantic network and the use of multiple colours to mark the lines [5]). Therefore, research with user involvement is being conducted to verify the usability of semantic network visualization as a user interface (this issue is widely discussed in [3]). These are the following publications:

- [25] - The main conclusions of their study are as follows: (1) the graph visualization is more controllable, intuitive and more suitable for overviews than indented tree hierarchies; (2) the graph visualization is more controllable and intuitive without visual redundancy, particularly for ontologies with multiple inheritances than indented tree hierarchies, and (3) the graph visualization is more suitable for overviews.
- [11] - The main conclusions of this study are as follows: (1) identification of potential problems related to the use of a semantic network as a visual interface in searching for economic information, which concern errors occurring during the ontology conceptualisation process for economic knowledge as well as the functionality of semantic network visualization software; (2) the application causes that users do not find it a problem that a semantic network contains many nodes and lines in many different colours.
- [43] - The main conclusions of this study are as follows: (1) information clearly presented by the system; (2) supporting the decision-making process; (3) the use of semantic analysis and complex networks as conjugated techniques can help in the decision-making process.

The four research areas specified in this section in relation to the application of semantic network visualization as a visual interface do not constitute separate groups.

3.3 Results of the Validation of Prototypes of the Created Ontology

We have been conducting research related to the use of semantic visualization for the analysis of business data. The purpose of our research is to present the potential applications of semantic visualization in management, which involves models of knowledge pertaining to the analysis of financial and economic indicators. This required creating ontologies for selected fields of economic knowledge. These ontologies were constructed using the approach presented in [44]. As of now, the following case studies have been developed:

- early warning system ontology [45];
- ontology of chosen financial indicators [46];
- Company's Liquidity ontology [47];
- ontology of emergency policy workflow [7];
- financial assessment ontology [48].

The created ontologies were coded using the Protégé software. Figure 1 presents a sample semantic visualization of business knowledge in the OntoGraf module in the Protégé software. This is the prototype of a financial assessment ontology.

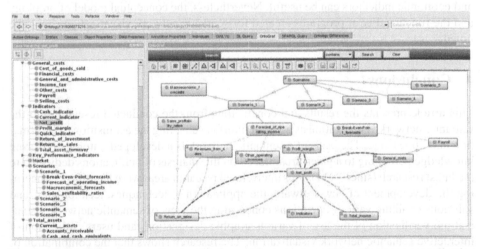

Fig. 1. An example of semantic visualization of business knowledge (Source: an application created on the basis of Protégé)

One of the stages of creating an ontology for a selected field of economic knowledge is the validation and evaluation stage of the created ontology. At this stage, the encoded ontology is checked to ensure that it meets the users' needs. Validation is carried out in three areas. Firstly, validation is performed by experts, who will potentially use it, with respect to the usefulness and correctness of the created ontology. Secondly, the evaluation of the application with the created ontology is carried out by users. Finally, the validation of predefined use cases is carried out.

At the stage of validation and evaluation, these case studies were tested by experts using pre-set usage scenarios. Several of them have been described in publications, for example [7, 46–48]. We prepared use cases and validated the created ontology. Experts searched for economic information using semantic network visualization in Protégé's OntoGraf module. Our goal concerning the OntoGraf module – which proved to be sufficient for the research – was to verify the usefulness of semantic network visualization in searching for business information that is contextually connected.

In the course of the validation of prototypes, two groups of problems were identified. The first group includes problems resulting from the ontology created. The most frequently reported problem concerned interpreting the names of semantic relations between concepts. This means that the usefulness of applying semantic network visualization depends on a good definition of semantic relations at the ontology conceptualization stage. The fundamental rule should be to use such relationship names that are understandable to users. Therefore, special attention should be paid to the ontology conceptualization stage. The second group includes problems related to software (in this case, the OntoGraf module in Protégé). The most frequently reported problem was the random arrangement of concepts in the visualization window e.g. after making the relationships expand or collapse.

To summarize, validation of prototypes of created ontologies confirmed that the application of semantic visualization as a visual interface for the analysis of financial and economic indicators can be useful. Nevertheless, the conceptual model of ontology and the functionality of programs created for semantic network visualization should be noted.

4   Conclusions

This article presents the results and conclusions from the conducted research into the semantic network visualization as a visual interface enabling the acquisition of information and knowledge. The basis of a semantic network is a developed ontology covering knowledge pertaining to a given area. Based on the analysis of publications dedicated to the latest research (since 2011), four interrelated research areas were identified, concerning the development of new software, the application of techniques, technologies, and solutions enabling various operations concerning the view of semantic network visualization, verification of the use of various graphic designations and users' validation of interactive semantic network visualization. The research shows that the combination of semantic network visualization and user navigation can be an effective and efficient tool for various analyses, including those of business data.

The conclusions from the encoding of ontologies for economic knowledge using the Protégé software as well as experts' testing of prototypes indicate the possibility of using a semantic network as a visual interface. The research confirms that semantic network visualization can be a useful visual interface for acquiring economic knowledge by users (managers). The combination of data visualization in the form of semantic network and personal navigation can become an effective and efficient tool to perform various analyses, including economic data. The research also aims at identifying potential problems associated with the use of semantic network visualization as a visual user interface. As a result of testing of the created ontologies, the following three groups of problems were identified. The first group concerns understanding the defined semantic relationships between concepts. The second group concerns understanding the operation of the software that displays semantic network visualization. The third group includes the functionality of the semantic visualization module. Finding solutions to minimize potential difficulties can contribute to the use of semantic visualization on a larger scale to represent economic knowledge in systems supporting decision-makers in making decisions.

Acknowledgements. The author would like to thank Jerzy Korczak from the International University of Logistics and Transport, Wrocław, Poland, and Bartłomiej Nita, and Piotr Oleksyk from Wrocław University of Economics, Wrocław, Poland for cooperation and their significant contribution to the development and validation of ontologies for financial knowledge.

References

1. Nazemi, K., Breyer, M., Burkhardt, D., Stab, C., Kohlhammer, J.: SemaVis: a new approach for visualizing semantic information. In: Wahlster, W., Grallert, H.-J., Wess, S., Friedrich, H., Widenka, T. (eds.) Towards the Internet of Services: The THESEUS Research Program. CT, pp. 191–202. Springer, Cham (2014). https://doi.org/10.1007/978-3-319-06755-1_15
2. Nazemi, K., Burkhardt, D., Ginters, E., Kohlhammer, J.: Semantics visualization – definition, approaches and challenges. Procedia Comput. Sci. Elsevier BV **75**, 75–83 (2015)
3. Nazemi, K.: Adaptive semantics visualization. In: Studies in Computational Intelligence, vol. 646, Springer, Cham (2016). https://doi.org/10.1007/978-3-319-30816-6
4. Chuprina, S., Nasraoui, O.: Using ontology-based adaptable scientific visualization and cognitive graphics tools to transform traditional information systems into intelligent systems. Sci. Visual. **8**(1), 23–44 (2016)
5. Hussain, A., Latif, K., Rextin, A.T., Hayat, A., Alam, M.: Scalable visualization of se-mantic nets using power-law graphs. Appl. Math. Inf. Sci. Int. J. **8**, 355–367 (2014). https://doi.org/10.12785/amis/080145
6. Aritonang, E., Seminar, K.B., Wahjuni, S., Purbo, O.W.: Modeling ontology and semantic network of regulations in customs and excise. TELKOMNIKA **15**(4), 1934–1942 (2018). https://doi.org/10.12928/telkomnika.v15i4.6590
7. Korczak, J., Dudycz, H., Nita, B., Oleksyk, P.: Semantic approach to financial knowledge specification - case of emergency policy workflow. In: Ziemba, E. (ed.) AITM/ISM -2017. LNBIP, vol. 311, pp. 24–40. Springer, Cham (2018). https://doi.org/10.1007/978-3-319-777 21-4_2
8. Krishnan, K., Krishnan, R., Muthumari, A.: A semantic-based ontology mapping–information retrieval for mobile learning resources. Int. J. Comput. Appl. **39**(3), 169–178 (2017). https://doi.org/10.1080/1206212X.2017.1309223
9. Selvalakshmi, B., Subramaniam, M.: Intelligent ontology based semantic information retrieval using feature selection and classification. Clust. Comput. **22**(5), 12871–12881 (2018). https://doi.org/10.1007/s10586-018-1789-8

10. Zhang, G., Li, Y.: Multiple disciplines product design knowledge representation strategy based on ontology and semantic network. TELKOMNIKA **11**(10), 6074–6079 (2013). https://doi.org/10.11591/telkomnika.v11i10.3467

11. Dudycz, H.: Usability of business information semantic network search visualization. In: Sikorski, M., Dittmar, A., Marasek, K., de Greef, T. (eds.) Proceedings of Multimedia, Interaction, Design and Innovation (MIDI 2015), ACM Digital Library, Article No. 13, pp. 1–9 (2015). https://doi.org/10.1145/2814464.2814477

12. Ward, M., Grinstein, G., Keim, D.: Interactive Data Visualization Foundations, Techniques, and Applications. Taylor & Francis Group, Boca Raton (2015)

13. Zhu, B., Chen, H.: Information visualization. Ann. Rev. Inf. Sci. Technol. **39**, 139–177 (2005). https://doi.org/10.1002/aris.1440390111

14. Burkhard, R.A., Meier, M.: Tube map visualization: evaluation of a novel knowledge visualization application for the transfer of knowledge in long-term projects. J. Univ. Comput. Sci. **11**(4), 473–494 (2005)

15. Lopes, A.A., Pinho, R., Paulovich, F.V., Minghim, R.: Visual text mining using association rules. Comput. Graph. **31**, 316–326 (2007)

16. Grand, B. L., Soto, M.: Topic maps, RDF graphs, and ontologies visualization. In: Geroimenko, V., Chen, C. (eds.) Visualizing the Semantic Web. XML-Based Internet and Information Visualization, pp. 59–79. Springer-Verlag, London (2010). https://doi.org/10.1007/1-84628-290-X

17. Wienhofen, L.W.M.: Using graphically represented ontologies for searching content on the semantic web. In: Geroimenko, V., Chen, C. (eds.) Visualizing the Semantic Web. XML-Based Internet and Information Visualization, pp. 137–153. Springer-Verlag, London (2010). https://doi.org/10.1007/1-84628-290-X

18. Eppler, M. E.: Facilitating knowledge communication through joint interactive visualization. J. Univ. Comput. Sci. **10**(6). 83–690 (2004)

19. Eppler, M.J., Burkhard, R.A.: Knowledge Visualization Towards a New Discipline and its Fields of Application. Universit'a della Svizzera Italiana, January (2004)

20. Azzi, R., Desprès, S., Nobécourt, J.: MCVGraphviz: a web tool for knowledge dynamic visualization. In: IEEE-RIVF International Conference on Computing and Communication Technologies (RIVF), pp. 1–6 (2019). https://doi.org/10.1109/RIVF.2019.8765697

21. Reeve,L., Han, H., Chen, C.: Information visualization and the semantic web. In: Geroimenko, V., Chen, C. (eds.) Visualizing the Semantic Web. XML-Based Internet and Information Visualization, pp. 19–44. London, Springer-Verlag (2010)

22. Arp, R., Smith, B., Spear, A.D.: Building Ontologies with Basic Formal Ontology, MIT Press, Cambridge (2015)

23. Achich, N., Bouaziz, B., Algergawy, A., Gargouri, F.: Ontology visualization: an overview. In: Abraham, A., Muhuri, P.K., Muda, A.K., Gandhi, N. (eds.) ISDA 2017. AISC, vol. 736, pp. 880–891. Springer, Cham (2018). https://doi.org/10.1007/978-3-319-76348-4_84

24. Dudáš, M., Lohmann, S., Svátek, V., Pavlov, D.: Ontology visualization methods and tools: a survey of the state of the art. Knowl. Eng. Rev. **33**, e10, 1–39 (2018). https://doi.org/10.1017/S0269888918000073

25. Fu, B., Noy, N.F., Storey, M.-A.: Indented tree or graph? a usability study of ontology visualization techniques in the context of class mapping evaluation. In: Alani, H., et al. (eds.) ISWC 2013. LNCS, vol. 8218, pp. 117–134. Springer, Heidelberg (2013). https://doi.org/10.1007/978-3-642-41335-3_8

26. Lanzenberger, M., Sampson, J., Rester, M.: Ontology visualization: tools and techniques for visual representation of semi-structured meta-data. J. Univ. Comput. Sci. **16**(7), 1036–1054 (2010). https://doi.org/10.3217/jucs-016-07-1036

27. Sivakumar, R., Arivoli, P.V.: Ontology visualization protégé tools – a review. Int. J. Adv. Inf. Technol. **1**, 4 (2011)

28. Ramakrishnan, S., Vijayan, A.: A study on development of cognitive support features in recent ontology visualization tools. Artif. Intell. Rev. **41**(4), 595–623 (2012). https://doi.org/ 10.1007/s10462-012-9326-2

29. Ertek, G., Tokdemir, G., Sevinç, M., Tunç, M.M.: New knowledge in strategic management through visually mining semantic networks. Inf. Syst. Front. **19**(1), 165–185 (2015). https:// doi.org/10.1007/s10796-015-9591-0

30. Fu, B., Noy, N.F., Storey, M.-A.: Eye tracking the user experience - an evaluation of ontology visualization techniques. Seman. Web **8**(1), 23–41 (2016). https://doi.org/10.3233/SW-140163

31. Moshref, M., Al-Sayyad, R.: Developing ontology approach using software tool to improve data visualization (Case Study: Computer Network). I. J. Mod. Educ. Comput. Sci. **4**, 32–39 (2019). https://doi.org/10.5815/ijmecs.2019.04.04

32. Khalili, A., Auer, S.: WYSIWYM – Integrated visualization, exploration and authoring of semantically enriched un-structured content. Seman. Web J. **6**(3), 259–275 (2014)

33. Korczak, J., Dudycz, H., Nita, B., Oleksyk, P.: Towards process-oriented ontology for financial analysis. In: Ganzha, M., Maciaszek, L., Paprzycki, M. (eds.) Proceedings of the 2017 Federated Conference on Computer Science and Information Systems. Annals of Computer Science and Information Systems, vol. 11, pp. 981–987 (2017). https://doi.org/10.15439/201 7F181

34. Stab, C., Nazemi, K., Breyer, M., Burkhardt, D., Kohlhammer, J.: Semantics visualization for fostering search result comprehension. In: Simperl, E., Cimiano, P., Polleres, A., Corcho, O., Presutti, V. (eds.) ESWC 2012. LNCS, vol. 7295, pp. 633–646. Springer, Heidelberg (2012). https://doi.org/10.1007/978-3-642-30284-8_49

35. Shneiderman, B.: The eyes have it: a task by data type taxonomy for information visualizations. In: Proceedings of the IEEE Symposium on Visual Languages, pp. 336–343 (1996)

36. Kitchenham, B.: Procedures for performing systematic reviews. Joint Technical Report, Keele: Keele University TR/SE-0401 and NICTA 0400011T.1, July (2004)

37. Nazemi, K., Breyer, M., Burkhardt, D., Fellner, D.W.: Visualization cock-pit: orchestration of multiple visualizations for knowledge-exploration. Int. J. Adv. Corp. Learn. **3**(4), 26–34 (2010)

38. Eisenstein, J., Chau, D.H., Kittur, A., Xing, E.: TopicViz: semantic navigation of document collections, arXiv preprint arXiv:1110.6200 1–14 (2011). https://arxiv.org/pdf/1110.6200.pdf

39. Burkhardt, D., Nazemi, K., Breyer, M., Stab, C., Kuijper, A.: SemaZoom: semantics exploration by using a layer-based focus and context metaphor. In: Kurosu, M. (ed.) HCD 2011. LNCS, vol. 6776, pp. 491–499. Springer, Heidelberg (2011). https://doi.org/10.1007/978-3-642-21753-1_55

40. Stab, C., Nazemi, K., Breyer, M., Burkhardt, D., Kuijper, A.: Interacting with semantics and time. In: Jacko, J.A. (ed.) HCI 2011. LNCS, vol. 6764, pp. 520–529. Springer, Heidelberg (2011). https://doi.org/10.1007/978-3-642-21619-0_64

41. Weiss, R.: MUCK: A toolkit for extracting and visualizing semantic dimensions of large text collections. In: Proceedings of the Workshop on Interactive Language Learning, Visualization, and Interfaces, pp. 53–58 (2014)

42. Larrea, M.L., Martig, S.R., Castro, S.M.: Semantics-based colour assignment in visualization. J. Comput. Sci. Technol. **10**, 1 (2010)

43. Lancellotta, P.I., Victor Ströele, V., Braga, R.M.M., David, J.M.N., Campos, F.: Semantic analysis and complex networks as conjugated techniques supporting decision making. In: 20th International Conference on Enterprise Information Systems ICEIS'2018, No. 2, pp.195–202 (2018). https://doi.org/10.5220/0006662001950202

44. Dudycz, H., Korczak, J.: Process of ontology design for business intelligence system. In: Ziemba, E. (ed.) Information Technology for Management. LNBIP, vol. 243, pp. 17–28. Springer, Cham (2016). https://doi.org/10.1007/978-3-319-30528-8_2
45. Dudycz, H.: Approach to the conceptualization of an ontology of an early warning system. In: Jałowiecki, P., Łukasiewicz, P., Orłowski, A. (eds.) Information Systems in Management XI. Data Bases, Distant Learning, and Web Solutions Technologies, No. XI, pp. 29–39 (2011)
46. Korczak, J., Dudycz, H., Dyczkowski, M.: Design of financial knowledge in dashboard for SME managers. In: Ganzha, M., Maciaszek, L., Paprzycki, M. (eds.) Proceedings of the 2013 Federated Conference on Computer Science and Information Systems. Annals of Computer Science and Information Systems, vol. 1, pp. 1111–1118 (2013)
47. Korczak, J., Dudycz, H., Nita, B., Oleksyk, P., Kaźmierczak, A.: Extension of intelligence of decision support systems: manager perspective. In: Ziemba, E. (ed.) AITM/ISM -2016. LNBIP, vol. 277, pp. 35–48. Springer, Cham (2017). https://doi.org/10.1007/978-3-319-530 76-5_3
48. Dudycz, H., Nita, B., Oleksyk, P.: Application of ontology in financial assessment based on real options in small and medium-sized companies. In: Ziemba, E. (ed.) AITM/ISM -2018. LNBIP, vol. 346, pp. 24–40. Springer, Cham (2019). https://doi.org/10.1007/978-3-030-151 54-6_2

Machine Learning Solutions in Retail eCommerce to Increase Marketing Efficiency

Maciej Pondel[1]([envelope]) [iD] and Jolanta Pondel[2] [iD]

[1] Wrocław University of Economics, Komandorska 118/120, Wrocław, Poland
maciej.pondel@ue.wroc.pl
[2] WSB University in Wrocław, Fabryczna St. 29-31, 53-609, Wrocław, Poland
jolanta.pondel@wsb.wroclaw.pl

Abstract. Retail companies operate in a highly competitive market. Marketing specialists should focus their activities on keeping customers loyalty on a high level, which is critical to achieving success in the retail business. The efficiency of marketing campaigns impacts the performance of the whole business directly. Electronic channels of customer contact help in gathering massive data sets describing customers and their behaviour. Companies can use the data to gain knowledge about their customers and valuable insights about patterns of customer behaviour. Such knowledge enables the application of actions improving the loyalty of customers and satisfaction of customers. This paper elaborates on customer loyalty and shows how to use data in marketing and sales processes in retail. Authors present a method of advanced data analysis based on machine learning techniques to generate tailored offers for clients applicable in an eCommerce company.

Keywords: Machine learning · Marketing · Retail · eCommerce · Customer churn

1 Introduction

Strong market competition and dynamic changes in the markets force enterprises to take actions directed at improving their relationships with customers. Those customers are increasingly choosing online stores as a place to buy (Doligalski 2018). The success of retail organisations depends on how adequately they can analyse the data about their clients' behaviour and draw valuable conclusions.

It is essential to acquire a new customer, but even more critical to keep the customer with good relation. The most critical priority impacting the future of the company and its financial results is to keep the customer satisfaction on a high level, improve the relationship with the customers and thus build long-term and profitable relationships. Such an approach requires many efforts to be taken, including financial and time engagements. It is also necessary to continually monitor the initiated activities, inspect the results, and take improving actions to ensure the conducted activities are proper and bring measurable benefits to the enterprise.

© IFIP International Federation for Information Processing 2021
Published by Springer Nature Switzerland AG 2021
M. L. Owoc and M. Pondel (Eds.): AI4KM 2019, IFIP AICT 599, pp. 91–105, 2021.
https://doi.org/10.1007/978-3-030-85001-2_8

The need to establish a lasting relationship with the customer becomes the foundation for market activities for enterprises, particularly in the retail market.

We can define customer loyalty as "… re-purchasing only one brand, without considering the purchase of other brands" (Newman and Werbel 1973) or as "… a persistent and consistent readiness to re-purchase or re-promote your preferred product or brand in the future, resulting in repeat purchases of the same brand despite market influences and marketing efforts that have the potential to change behaviour" (Oliver 1999). Two aspects of loyalty can be distinguished based on the definition:

- a behavioural aspect related to specific behaviours,
- the emotional element, expressed by the customer's attachment and "… attitude towards specific objects related to the supplier, leading to the expression of loyalty behaviour"(Urban and Siemieniako 2008).

There is also an essential phenomenon of emotional attachment, also called "the cli-ent's emotional loyalty". Customers with apparent loyalty are more susceptible to changing the supplier under the influence of favourable economic factors, and reshopping is not related to the positive attitude of the customer and how they are devoted to the company. An essential feature of loyalty is that the purchase is planned, not accidental. Loyalty is the result of a deliberate choice, not a case or alternative offer (Bloomer and Kasper 1995).

Customer loyalty is closely related to their satisfaction. A satisfied customer is likely to make purchases again. Satisfaction is a prerequisite, but not always enough to achieve true loyalty (Sudolska 2011). Research shows that among customers who decide to change suppliers, about 65–85% are satisfied with the received product (Stum and Thirty 1991). The relationship between satisfaction and loyalty depends on the degree of competition in a given market. To maintain the customer and provide them with favourable conditions, the company must measure customer loyalty and customer satisfaction.

The full availability of communication and sales channels provided by the Internet and social media has radically changed the traditional buying model. Customers expect a higher and higher quality of service and convenience provided by the eCommerce channel. It is essential in such an approach to allow customers to interact in a convenient way and at the time they prefer. Additional occasions, such as providing tools and information, allow building even closer relations.

Rawson states that many companies excel in individual interactions with customers, but they fail to pay adequate attention to the customer's complete experience on the way to purchase and after. Solution for the problem is that companies need to combine top-down, judgment-driven evaluations and bottom-up, data-driven analysis to identify key journeys, and then engage the entire organization in redesigning the customer experience. This requires shifting from siloed to cross-functional approaches and changing from a touchpoint to a journey orientation (Rawson et al. 2013).

An important factor determining customer's satisfaction and loyalty is the personalization of approach and customized offers directed to clients. To be able to generate such, the company must conduct in-depth and multidimensional customer analysis.

The main goal of this paper is to elaborate customers loyalty and satisfaction and known methods involving the acquisition of knowledge about customers to apply a customized approach to a client. This paper's aim is also to propose the innovative method of B2C eCommerce originated data analysis to generate recommendations of marketing actions.

This paper is structured as follows. In the next section, the related articles are analyzed and basing on other research findings, authors provide the foundation of the proposed data analysis method. The research gap is also identified. The following section describes research method and next the results of research are presented, and the results are discussed.

2 Related Works

Techniques of collecting information from clients can be based, for example, on the surveys, interviews, reports, or direct conversations with customers. You can use for this (Jones and Sasser 1995; Ciok 2006):

- customer satisfaction indicators,
- questionnaire surveys,
- feedback from the customer (comments, complaints and questions from customers),
- market research,
- staff who have direct contact with the client,
- strategic activities (hiring employees in the same market as the target group, inviting clients to work related to the improvement of products and services,
- apparent shopping (mysterious customer),
- analysis of customer loss (contact with customers who stopped buying products to identify the problem).

However, the information obtained from these sources may be biased, as the customers may not want to express their real opinion (fear, lack of time, different perception of product or service). Authors of this paper would like to elaborate on different sources of data storing recorded real actions of all customers to analyze the whole range of customers and acquire actual shopping patterns.

The problem of customer-related data analysis is widely discussed in the literature. Most of the applications regard to customer churn (Burez and Van den Poel 2009; De Caigny et al. 2018). Customer churn (Amin et al. 2019) is commonly related to service industries, and rarely considered as a problem in eCommerce-oriented retail sector.

Customers who stop using products/services of the company are considered as churn customers. We consider customers' churn as a lost opportunity for profit. One of the main reasons to undergo the customer's preservation process is that keeping a customer is far less expensive than finding a new customer. That is, the sale cost for new customers is five times of that of old customers (Fathian et al. 2016). Bhattacharya claims that the cost of obtaining a new customer is usually five to even six times higher than the costs of retaining an existing one (Bhattacharya 1998).

As a result, efforts done by marketing specialists to sustain market share switched from focusing on acquiring new customers to retaining existing - reducing customer churn. For this reason, customer churn, also known as customer turnover, customer attrition, or customer deflection, is a significant concern for several industries. That is why customer churn is especially relevant in the e-commerce context, where consumers can easily compare products or services and change the merchant with minimal effort. Therefore, by spotting churned customers and understanding drivers, companies may have a better chance to minimize customers' churn.

During the last decade, customer churn prediction has received a growing consideration in order to survive in an increasingly competitive and global marketplace (Gordini 2017). Concretely, in customer churn prediction, a scoring model allows the estimation of a future churn probability for every customer based on the historical knowledge of the customer. In practice, these scores can be used to select targeted customers for a retention campaign (De Caigny et al. 2018).

We can find several approaches for telecom industry (Amin et al. 2019; Hung et al. 2006; Lu et al. 2012; Tsai and Lu 2009) financial industry (banking and insurance) (Zhao and Dang 2008; Prasad and Madhavi 2012), subscription services like pay-TV (Burez and Van den Poel 2007) and cellular network services (Sharma et al. 2013). In service industries like those mentioned, the definition of customer churn is clear. There is usually a contract between customer and service provider. When such a contract expires or is terminated, we can clearly say that customer abandoned company (is a churned customer). Few publications elaborating on churn analysis in retail business can be found. In (Yu et al. 2011) we can find a recommendation to predict eCommerce customer churn based on SVM algorithm. A practical drawback of such approach is a premise that we can apply binary classification (churn and non-churn) while eCommerce reality is much more complicated. In retail and eCommerce, we focus more on customer recency than churn. It is difficult to identify the exact moment when clients discontinue their relationship with companies (Miguéis et al. 2012). If a customer has not placed an order for 100 days, we cannot clearly state that he or she is a churned customer. We can only predict the probability or the customer's return. In (Miguéis et al. 2012) we can find an interesting approach based on sequence mining. Authors grouped the purchases in periods of three months and by classifying as churners those customers who, from a certain period, did not buy anything else or those who in all subsequent periods spent less than 40% of the amount spent in the reference period. Companies should strive for models that can accurately identify potential churners, and this becomes even more important in the digital economy context. Over the last decade, this issue was mentioned and researched by many practitioners and academics.

In the present literature, we can observe two main trends concerning customer churn. According to (Gordini 2017) the first branch includes traditional classification methods such as decision tree and logistic regression (Burez and Van den Poel 2007; Gordini and Veglio 2013, 2014; Verbeke et al. 2011). Next approach is based on the artificial intelligence methods such as neural networks (Gordini and Veglio, 2013; Sharma et al. 2013).

In (Sulistiani and Tjahyanto 2017) we can find an experiment concerning the prediction of customer loyalty based on a data gathered from customer survey where they declare their satisfaction, but as mentioned earlier, this paper concentrates on researching real customer's behavior rather than their declarations.

There are several factors impacting customer loyalty in eCommerce. One of them is the customization of offers. In (Clauss et al. 2018) the factor is listed among such as reliability, price value, information quality, and others. Personalization of offers is understood as a positive answer to the following questions:

- This platform makes purchase recommendations that match my needs.
- The advertisements and promotions that this platform sends to me are tailored to my situation.
- I believe that this platform is customized to my needs.

In (Pappas et al. 2017) authors identify personalization as an essential factor in the area of marketing. Online shopping personalization is a strategy that may aid in persuading customers to select a product or service and lead to a purchase. The conclusion is that a key factor in increasing customer loyalty is a proper personalisation, but authors also claim that traditional techniques in personalized online shopping (e.g., recommendations based on previous purchases, tailored messages based on browsing history) are not enough to lead customers to an online purchase, when customers are on a shopping mission. Importance of identification of customer's price sensitivity and promotion sensitivity in building positive customer experience and loyalty is also highlighted.

The positive recommendation based algorithms are used in a vast amount of websites, such as the movie recommendation algorithms on Netflix, the music recommendations on Spotify, video recommendations on Youtube and the product recommendations on Amazon (Boström and Filipsson 2017). Online product recommendation mechanism is becoming increasingly available on websites to assist consumers in reducing information overload, provide advice in finding suitable products, and facilitate online consumer decision-making. Recommendation mechanisms have been found to help consumers efficiently filter available alternatives, increase the quality of their consideration set and increase their product choice satisfaction (Lee and Kwon 2008).

In this paper, authors concentrate on methods preventing customer churn by purchase patterns detection combined with customer segmentation to define best suited marketing messages and tailored offers adjusted to actual customer's needs and expectations to build positive experience increasing loyalty.

3   Research Method

The most common methods of data analysis used in marketing are:

- Frequent Pattern Mining (Association rules and sequence rules).
- Collaborative Filtering.
- Clustering.
- Classification and regression.

The concept of frequent itemset was first introduced for mining transaction databases (Han et al. 2007). Frequent patterns are itemsets, subsequences, or substructures that appear in a data set with frequency no less than a user-specified threshold. Frequent pattern mining was first proposed by Agrawal et al. (1993) for market basket analysis in the form of association rule mining. It analyses customer buying habits by finding associations between the different items that customers place in their "shopping baskets". There are many algorithms searching for association rules such as Apriori, Charm, FP-Growth and others. They differ in computational complexity, and thus in resource demand and execution time. Their operation is deterministic, so the obtained results will be the same. The source data for association rules is a set of transactions/orders of a customer in eCommerce store. The analysis is also referred to as "Market basket analysis" because it searches for patterns in shopping baskets. The result of an algorithm is a list of frequent sets (products appearing frequently). Having a list of sets we are able to construct rules answering a question which products are frequently purchased together. Example of association rules generated using FP-Growth algorithm is presented in Fig. 1.

First product	Next product	Confidence	Frequency ▼	Lift
Calvin Klein / Gloves and scarves / Unisex	Calvin Klein / Winter hats / Unisex	32,13%	392	17,08
Calvin Klein / Winter hats / Unisex	Calvin Klein / Gloves and scarves / Unisex	17,21%	392	17,08
Calvin Klein / Shirts / Women	DKNY / Shirts / Women	20,55%	598	10,10
DKNY / Shirts / Women	Calvin Klein / Shirts / Women	24,28%	598	10,10
DKNY / Socks / Unisex	Lauren / Socks / Unisex	9,68%	224	9,72
Lauren / Socks / Unisex	DKNY / Socks / Unisex	18,59%	224	9,72
DKNY / Socks / Unisex	DKNY / Socks / Women	6,48%	150	9,54
DKNY / Socks / Women	DKNY / Socks / Unisex	18,25%	150	9,54

Fig. 1. Example of association rules

Each rule is evaluated by the following measures:

Confidence – this is a percentage value that shows the probability of consequent product purchase in a situation where an antecedent product has been already placed in a basket.

Frequency – number of transactions including both products. It helps to asses if a rule is common or perhaps is only an exception. If confidence is high and frequency is low, it means that two very seldom bought products were purchased together only a few times. In such case, the overall value of a rule is considered as low.

Lift – this is the ratio determining independence of antecedent and consequent product. In some cases, confidence and frequency are not enough to evaluate a rule. If e.g. a plastic bag is added to nearly all orders, the rules with a plastic bag as a consequent product will have a very high confidence as well as high frequency, but the business value of those rules will be very low. To eliminate those rules from further considering lift can help. If the rule had a lift of 1, it would imply that the probability of occurrence of the antecedent and that of the consequent are independent of each other. When two events are independent of each other, no rule can be drawn involving those two events. If the lift is > 1, that lets us know the degree to which those two occurrences are dependent on one another and makes those rules potentially useful for predicting the consequent in future data sets. If the lift is < 1, that lets us know the items are a substitute to each other. This means that the presence of one item has a negative effect on the presence of another item and vice versa.

There are more measures to value the association rule like support, coverage, strength or leverage. In our experiment, we find it enough to analyze those 3 measures explained and presented in Fig. 1.

Sequence rules algorithm is based on a similar foundation. A sequence database consists of ordered elements or events, recorded with or without a concrete notion of time. There are many applications involving sequence data, such as customer shopping sequences, Web clickstreams, and biological sequences.

Agrawal and Srikant first introduced the sequential pattern mining in (Srikant and Agrawal 1996). Given a set of sequences, where each sequence consists of a list of elements and each element consists of a set of items, and given a user-specified minsupport threshold, sequential pattern mining is to find all the frequent subsequences, i.e., the subsequences whose occurrence frequency in the set of sequences is no less than minsupport.

The result of sequence mining is a list of rules valued with similar measures like in case of association rules. The most important difference is that sequence mining help with the prediction of future purchases of customers basing on their previously bought products. Antecedent and consequent products may be the same in a situation where customers regularly buys the same products that end or wear out and then need to be re-purchsed. In case of association rules such situation never happens. One product cannot be purchased together with itself. If customer buys a several items of the same product it is treated by algorithm as one product.

Example of sequence rules generated by PrefixSpan algorithm is presented in Fig. 2.

Antecedent	Consequent	Frequency	Confidence	Support
Hilfiger / Shirts / Men	Calvin Klein / Shirts / Men	174	14,09%	0,064%
Calvin Klein / Polo shirts / Men	Calvin Klein / Shirts / Men	208	13,00%	0,076%
Calvin Klein / Shirts / Men	Calvin Klein / Shirts / Men	1237	11,78%	0,453%
Calvin Klein / Polo shirts / Men	Calvin Klein / Sweatshirts / Men	168	10,50%	0,062%
Versace / Shirts / Men	Calvin Klein / Shirts / Men	145	10,36%	0,053%
DKNY / Shirts / Men	Calvin Klein / Shirts / Men	748	10,35%	0,274%
Calvin Klein / Autumn jackets / Men	Calvin Klein / Shirts / Men	262	9,72%	0,096%
Calvin Klein / Shorts / Men	Calvin Klein / Shirts / Men	347	9,53%	0,127%
Calvin Klein / Polo shirts / Men	DKNY / Shirts / Men	147	9,19%	0,054%
DKNY / Shirts / Men	DKNY / Shirts / Men	646	8,94%	0,236%
Calvin Klein / Autumn jackets / Men	Calvin Klein / Sweatshirts / Men	239	8,87%	0,087%
DKNY / Polo shirts / Men	Calvin Klein / Shirts / Men	144	8,79%	0,053%
Calvin Klein / Sweatshirts / Men	Calvin Klein / Sweatshirts / Men	923	8,73%	0,338%

Fig. 2. Sequence rules generated by PrefixSpan algorithm

Collaborative Filtering is the process of filtering or evaluating items using the opinions of other people (Schafer et al. 2007).

Collaborative Filtering is the most widely used technique for Recommender Systems. The biggest advantage of Collaborative Filtering over content-based systems is that explicit content description is not required. Instead Collaborative Filtering only relies on opinions expressed by users on items. Instead of calculating the similarity between an item description and a user profile as a content-based recommender would do, a Collaborative Filtering system searches for similar users (neighbours) and then uses ratings from this set of users to predict items that will be liked by the current user (Massa and Avesani 2004).

Unfortunately, in regular eCommerce in contrast to content delivery services (music or movie providers) users are not used to express opinions about the product they have purchased that is why collaborative filtering has limited usage in the topic of this paper.

The goal of clustering is to find clusters of similar observations in a set of customers, products, transactions, and customer contacts with store web pages. In our experiment, we would like to determine segments of customers to whom we can send an offer or whom we can target when promoting specific products. We require clusters to have specific statistical characteristics (such as minimum variance) and usefulness in marketing decision making (e.g. determining loyal customer groups).

There are several algorithms supporting clustering. In our experiments we concentrate on the following:

k-means based on the Euclidean distance between observations, Bisecting k-means acting on a similar basis to k-means, however, starting with all the observations in one cluster and then dividing the cluster into 2 sub-clusters, using the k-means algorithm,

Gaussian Mixture Model (GMM), which is a probabilistic model based on the assumption that a particular feature has a finite number of normal distributions, DBSCAN identifying clusters by measuring density as the number of observations in the designated area. If the density is greater than the density of observations belonging to other clusters, then the defined area is identified as a cluster.

To define the goal of customer clustering, we used RFM method widely used in the marketing of retail companies. The acronym RFM comes from the words "recency" (a period from the last purchase), "frequency", and "monetary value". In this type of analysis, customers are divided into groups, based on information on time which has passed from last purchases, how often they make purchases, and how much money they spent.

The following observations explain why RFM is interesting for retail companies:

• Customers who have recently made purchases are more likely to make a new purchase soon.
• Customers who frequently make purchases are more likely to do more shop-ping.
• Customers who spend a lot of money are more likely to spend more money. Each of these observations corresponds to one of the dimensions of RFM.

An example of RFM clustering is presented in Fig. 3. One customer is one dot and color presents the number of a cluster to which customer was assigned.

Another set of characteristics describing customer behaviour was used in the next experiment. Personal interviews with eCommerce managers inspired another proposed segmentation. Mangers autonomously observed two major in terms of profit generation but also contrary segments of customers. One of the segments brings together fashion-driven customers (they are interested in mainly new and fashionable items). The second one is "bargain hunters" – discount-driven customers who are eager to purchase products present on the market for a longer time, but they expect significantly high discounts. This segmentation is referred to as "fashion vs. discount". In such segmentation we take into account the following dimensions:

Segment ● 1 ● 2 ● 3 ○ 4 ● 5 ○ 6

Fig. 3. RFM clustering using k-means algorithm.

- Average discount of a customer.
- The average number of days from product launch to transaction.
- Average order value.
- Number of orders.

The distribution of average discount used by a customer in their transactions is presented in Fig. 4. Another dimension showing if customers purchase new or relatively old products is shown in Fig. 5. Those graphs present that there are customers (cluster no 5) where the average discount is 2% only, which means that in fact, they do not expect any discount. At the same time, they buy relatively new products so we can state that cluster 5 is fashion-driven. The opposite clusters are 1 and 4. Those clients expect about 50% discount, which is exceptionally high, and they buy old products so they can be referred to as "bargain hunters". Every identified segment of customers expect separate pricing policy to achieve customer satisfaction when it comes to response for the offer.

To provide the customer with an attractive offer, we have to classify the user in terms of the advertised product and the proposed purchase conditions (price, discount, additional value). Many marketers are moving away from traditional aggregate-level mass marketing programs and are searching for accurate methods of identifying their most promising customers to focus specifically on those individuals (Kaefer et al. 2005). In contrast to the mass marketing approach, a direct marketing approach evaluates the profitability of current and potential customers and uses this information to focus marketing resources on their best prospects. Various studies have found that a consumer's past purchases can act as a good predictor of future preferences and choice outcomes. Classification is a technique where we categorize data into a given number of classes (e.g. purchasing/non-purchasing category). The main goal of a classification problem is to identify the category/class to which a new data should be assigned, basing on the whole

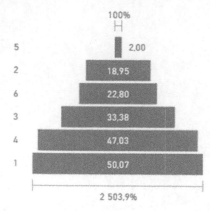

Fig. 4. Average discount distribution among clusters of customers.

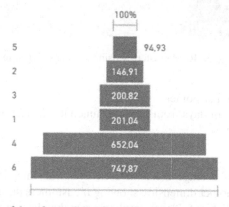

Fig. 5. Average number of days from product launch to transaction distribution between clusters.

available characteristic of customers (demographic profile, previously purchased products, selected conditions). The most challenging issue in preparation of the classification model is to choose correct features to train a model.

4   Results of the Research

Our research aims to find a method enabling providing each customer of internet store most accurate offer in terms of:

- product category,
- price level,
- discount level,
- moment in time to buy.

Such a proposal generation considers the history of customer purchases. We analyze what products he or she has purchased, but also the conditions of the purchase (price and discount). Among the whole population of customers, we are searching for purchase patterns. Those patterns are identified separately for various subsets of the population, e.g. we identify them for both genders separately, but those subsets are also based on other demographic characteristics that we can identify. Having eCommerce data in most cases, we know the customer's gender as well as location (delivery place), but we do not know the customer's age.

To achieve such accurate proposal the combination of previously mentioned methods is required.

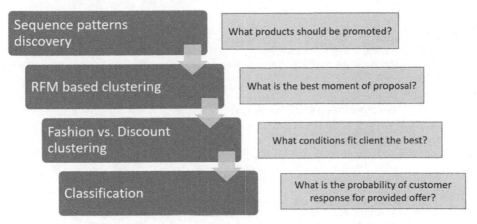

Fig. 6. Procedure to predict of the best offer for a customer.

The procedure of the tailored offer generation for each individual customer is proposed in Fig. 6. Basing on the first 3 steps we generate various options for proproposals. Lasts step (the classification model) is used to evaluate generated offers and selected only this/those with highest probability. The step is to avoid the situation where customer is overwhelmed with delivered offers. We would like to provide them with accurate number of messages not to discourage them.

In the last stage we build classification models where the target variable takes values: will buy/will not buy. The classification model is always generated in the context of a product category that was pointed out by sequence rules. In that case, we know that there is an evident reference between the historical purchases and a current one.

Such an approach generates several classification models depending on the number of sequence rules that have been discovered. We train every model using the data of customers who bought product categories indicated as an antecedent of a sequence rule (their demographic profile, history of orders) and analyze if they have purchased the consequent product. Such an approach predicts the recommended product more accurate than only sequence rules because it includes the context of each individual customer.

The moment in time for offer delivery and proposed conditions in terms of discount result from the clustering applied to a customer.

Classification algorithm selected for this task is XGBoost, which is nowadays considered as very efficient and has been widely recognized in many machine learning and data mining challenges (Chen and Guestrin 2016). This algorithm uses a gradient tree boosting technique.

Having trained and tested algorithm, we can apply it on every single customer data to estimate the probability of a selected product category to be purchased by a given client. As we can see in Fig. 7, such an approach for rules with 8% confidence was validated in case of a specific client to give us more than 40% probability of a customer's next purchase.

Customer	Antecedent	Rule confidence	Customer purchase probability
4b8e9135013449fbc572622f3 a1fa5ac@unity.pl	DKNY / Sweatshirts / Women	5,041%	48,900%
12fdedad5670aa94cc236df62 592bd8d@unity.pl	DKNY / Sweatshirts / Women	5,041%	48,700%
23b07a69b044c4381d329a71 6f0a3152@unity.pl	DKNY / Trousers / Women	6,714%	48,400%
20bf61d7ffd975b7d69289fd9 c922852@unity.pl	Lauren / Socks / Unisex	8,285%	47,500%
d51a6cb734ee215e2e66d39e 3ca7d7c0@unity.pl	Lauren / Socks / Unisex	8,285%	44,900%
05996c40624b776c6fed8077 1e6f6312@unity.pl	Lauren / Socks / Unisex	8,285%	44,800%
9a5453c0fb7043be3899e79c 924af0e8@unity.pl	Lauren / Socks / Unisex	8,285%	44,800%
266421292d70aa3936079f75 cb14956e@unity.pl	Lauren / Socks / Unisex	8,285%	44,300%
cc30a9f4a7dfcd480a4faccf84 8c4538@unity.pl	Lauren / Socks / Unisex	8,285%	44,300%
e6212112d8ecb6f1796db4b7 52b59794@unity.pl	Lauren / Socks / Unisex	8,285%	44,300%
09332ea8b8442cd3f9e18f075 0be2285@unity.pl	Calvin Klein / Lifestyle shoes / Women	4,877%	43,300%

Fig. 7. Results of classification algorithm applied of a list of customers

Having that knowledge, we can prepare a tailored offer for every single customer. The proposed approach seems to give valuable insights regarding marketing activities. Authors will validate the real business value of the proposed method in the next phases of this research study.

5 Discussion

eCommerce is a very efficient sale channel for both retailers and their customers. Due to its convenience customers can easily switch between providers. Well adjusted offers and personalization can be considered as a critical factor in the process of building long-lasting relationships that limit customer churn phenomenon. The proposed method of combining several machine learning techniques in one comprehensive process for tailored offers generation brings promising results. Purchase probability rated for 40% is very high. When we compare it to the average conversion rate is between 1% and 4% (Digitalmarketinginstitute 2020), the achieved number is impressive. We have to remember that predicted probability cannot be treated as expected campaign conversion rate. Several factors lower the final conversion (customer may miss the offer; they can purchase from other vendor and others). Such a method was tested in experimental campaigns resulted in 4 times higher Click-through rate and 3 times higher conversion when comparing to traditional campaign prepared by marketing analysts. Those results prove that the proposed approach can be efficient. Further research will be concentrated on tuning and adjusting the method to achieve higher efficiency of campaigns. Another direction of work will regard to store and include Big Data use cases including web events like clicks, page views, searches and others.

6 Conclusions

Data analysis based on machine learning can be applied in marketing and customerrelated data. The topic is widely discussed in the literature however research regards mostly to customer churn problem and in terms of customer segmentation, satisfaction, and loyalty base on surveys and more psychological grounds. Authors proposed the method of data analysis that is a combination of various techniques and algorithms of machine learning that is aimed to give a better result than typical methods to raise customer loyalty in the retail business.

References

1. Agrawal, R., Imieliński, T., Swami, A.: Mining association rules between sets of items in large databases. In: ACM Sigmod Record (vol. 22, no. 2). ACM (1993)
2. Amin, A., et al.: Cross-company customer churn prediction in telecommunication: a comparison of data transformation methods. Int. J. Inf. Manage. **46**, 304–319 (2019)
3. Bhattacharya, C.B.: When customers are members: customer retention in paid membership contexts. J. Acad. Mark. Sci. **26**(1), 31–44 (1998)
4. Bloemer, J.M.M., Kasper, H.D.P.: The complex relationship between consumer satisfaction and brand loyalty. J. Econ. Psychol. **16**, 311–329 (1995)
5. Boström, P., Filipsson, M.: comparison of user based and item based collaborative filtering recommendation services (2017)
6. Burez, J., Van den Poel, D.: CRM at a pay-TV company: using analytical models to reduce customer attrition by targeted marketing for subscription services. Exp. Syst. Appl. **32**(2), 277–288 (2007)
7. Burez, J., Van den Poel, D.: Handling class imbalance in customer churn prediction. Exp. Syst. Appl. **36**(3), 4626–4636 (2009)
8. Chen, T., Guestrin, C.: Xgboost: A scalable tree boosting system. In Proceedings of the 22nd ACM SIGKDD International Conference on Knowledge Discovery and Data Mining. ACM (2016)
9. Ciok, E.: Trust, but control basic information about Mystery Shopping (pol. Ufaj, ale kontroluj -czyli podstawowe informacje na temat Mystery Shopping), Zarządzanie jakością, nr 1 (2006)
10. Clauss, T., Harengel, P., Hock, M.: The perception of value of platform-based business models in the sharing economy: determining the drivers of user loyalty. RMS **13**(3), 605–634 (2018). https://doi.org/10.1007/s11846-018-0313-0
11. De Caigny, A., Coussement, K., De Bock, K.W.: A new hybrid classification algorithm for customer churn prediction based on logistic regression and decision trees. Eur. J. Oper. Res. **269**(2), 760–772 (2018)

12. Doligalski T.: E-commerce 2018 convenience of customers, sweat and tears of sellers (pol. E-commerce 2018 – wygoda klientów, pot i łzy sprzedawców), Gazeta SGH (2018)
13. https://digitalmarketinginstitute.com/blog/what-is-a-good-conversion-rate-for-ecommerce. Accessed 8 Jan 2020
14. Fathian, M., Hoseinpoor, Y., Minaei-Bidgoli, B.: Offering a hybrid approach of data mining to predict the customer churn based on bagging and boosting methods. Kybernetes 45(5) (2016)
15. Gordini, N.: Market driven management. A critical literature overview. Symph. Emerg. Iss. Manag. 2, 97–109 (2017). https://doi.org/10.4468/2010.2.08gordini
16. Gordini, N., Veglio, V.: Using neural networks for customer churn predictionmod-eling: preliminary findings from the Italian electricity industry In: Proceedings de X° Convegno Annuale della Società Italiana Marketing: "Smart Life. Dall'Innovazione Tecnologica al Mercato", 3–4 Ottobre 2013. Università degli Studi di Milano-Bicocca, Milano (2013)
17. Han, J., Cheng, H., Xin, D., Yan, X.: Frequent pattern mining: current status and future directions. Data Min. Knowl. Disc. 15(1), 55–86 (2007)
18. Hung, S.Y., Yen, D.C., Wang, H.Y.: Applying data mining to telecom churn management. Exp. Syst. Appl. 31(3), 55–86 (2006)
19. Jones, T.O., Sasser, W.E.: Why satisfied customers defect, Harward Bus. Rev. nr 6 (1995)
20. Kaefer, F., Heilman, C.M., Ramenofsky, S.D.: A neural network application to consumer classification to improve the timing of direct marketing activities. Comput. Oper. Res. 32(10), 2595–2615 (2005)
21. Lee, K.C., Kwon, S.: Online shopping recommendation mechanism and its influence on consumer decisions and behaviors: a causal map approach. Exp. Syst. Appl. 35(4), 1567–1574 (2008)
22. Lu, N., Lin, H., Lu, J., Zhang, G.: A customer churn prediction model in telecom industry using boosting. IEEE Trans. Ind. Inf. 10(2), 1659–1665 (2012)
23. Massa, P., Avesani, P.: Trust-aware collaborative filtering for recommender systems. In: Meersman, R., Tari, Z. (eds.) OTM 2004. LNCS, vol. 3290, pp. 492–508. Springer, Heidelberg (2004). https://doi.org/10.1007/978-3-540-30468-5_31
24. Miguéis, V.L., Van den Poel, D., Camanho, A.S., Cunha, J.F.: Modeling partial customer churn: On the value of first product-category purchase sequences. Exp. Syst. Appl. 39(12) (2012)
25. Newman, J.W., Werbel, R.A.: Analysis of brand loyalty for major household appliances. J. Mark. Res. 10, 404–409 (1973)
26. Oliver, R.L.: Whence consumer loyalty, J. Market. 63, 33– 44 (1999)
27. Pappas, I.O., Kourouthanassis, P.E., Giannakos, M.N., Lekakos G.: The interplay of online shopping motivations and experiential factors on personalized e-commerce: a complexity theory approach. Telemat. Infor. 34(5), 730–742 (2017)
28. Prasad, U.D., Madhavi S.: Prediction of churn behavior of bank customers using da-ta mining tools. Bus. Intell. J. 5(1) (2012)
29. Rawson, A., Duncan, E., Jones C.: The truth about customer experience. Harvard Bus. Rev. 91(9) (2013)
30. Schafer, J.B., Frankowski, D., Herlocker, J., Sen, S.: Collaborative filtering recommender systems. In: Brusilovsky, P., Kobsa, A., Nejdl, W. (eds.) The Adaptive Web. Lecture Notes in Computer Science, vol. 4321. Springer, Berlin (2007). https://doi.org/10.1007/978-3-540-72079-9_9
31. Sharma, A., Panigrahi, D., Kumar, P.: A neural network based approach for predicting customer churn in cellular network services. arXiv preprint (2013)
32. Srikant, R., Agrawal, R.: Mining sequential patterns: Generalizations and performance improvements. In: Apers, P., Bouzeghoub, M., Gardarin, G. (eds.) EDBT 1996. LNCS, vol. 1057, pp. 1–17. Springer, Heidelberg (1996). https://doi.org/10.1007/BFb0014140

33. Stum, D., Thiry, A.: Building customer loyalty, Train. Dev. J. **34** (1991)
34. Sudolska, A.: Managing customer experience as a key factor in the process of building their loyalty (pol. Zarządzanie doświadczeniem klientów jako kluczowy czynnik w procesie budowania ich lojalności), Zeszyty Naukowe Uniwersytetu Szczecińskiego nr660, Ekonomiczne problemy usług nr 72, Uniwersytet Szczeciński, Szczecin (2011)
35. Sulistiani, H., Tjahyanto, A.: Comparative analysis of feature selection method to predict customer loyalty. IPTEK J. Eng. **3**(1) (2017)
36. Tsai, C.F., Lu, Y.H.: Customer churn prediction by hybrid neural networks. Exp. Syst. Appl. **36**(10), 12547–12553 (2009)
37. Urban, W., Siemieniako, D.: Customer Loyalty. Models, Motivation and Measurement (pol. Lojalność klientów. Modele, motywacja i pomiar), PWN, Warszawa (2008)
38. Verbeke, W., Martens, D., Mues, C., Baesens, B.: Building comprehensible customer churn prediction models with advanced rule induction techniques. Exp.Syst. Appl. **38**(3), 2354–2364 (2011). https://doi.org/10.1016/j.eswa.2010.08.023
39. Yu, X., Guo, S., Guo, J., Huang, X.: An extended support vector machine forecasting framework for customer churn in e-commerce. Exp. Syst. Appl. **38**(3), 1425–1430 (2011)
40. Zhao, J., Dang, X.H.: Bank customer churn prediction based on support vector ma-chine: taking a commercial bank's VIP customer churn as the example. In: 2008 4th International Conference on Wireless Communications, Networking and Mobile Computing, IEEE (2008)

Author Index

Printed in the United States
by Baker & Taylor Publisher Services

Printed in the United States
by Baker & Taylor Publisher Services